The Organising Committee

greatly appreciates the contribution of

Elizabeth Pascoe

to the

1999 New Zealand Law Conference

in Rotorua, New Zealand

Doug Clemens
Conference Convenor

Paul Heath QC
Sessions Convenor

SIMPLY

NEW ZEALAND

A CULINARY JOURNEY

SIMPLY
NEW ZEALAND
A CULINARY JOURNEY

C. J. Publishing/Viking

ACKNOWLEDGMENTS

In the course of producing this book, we visited many places that were not well known to us. We were dependent on word-of-mouth recommendations from local people to steer us in the direction of their favourite eating spots. We extend our warmest thanks for guiding us to what we think are some of the finest eateries in the country at this time. Special thanks go to Ian Baker for his enthusiasm and hard work in completing the photography and collecting (and tasting!) the recipes from the various restaurants and cafés.

To Jan Bilton, Dexter Fry, Pamela Parsons, Sue Attwood and to Mary Dobbyn, Jeannetta Josephs and Jeanne-Maree Fitzgerald, a sincere thanks. Most of all, our thanks go to the owners and chefs of the New Zealand restaurants who participated in our first culinary journey.

Cover photo: Canterbury Tales. This baked salmon recipe comes from Hamilton. See page 64.

Publisher: Cliff Josephs
Editor: Pamela Parsons
Food Editor: Jan Bilton
Editorial Assistant: Mary Dobbyn
Design and Production: Dexter Fry
Design Associate: Sue Attwood
Photography: Ian Baker and contributors
Printed by Bookbuilders, Hong Kong

C. J. Publishing

Edited, designed and produced by

C. J. Publishing, P O Box 403, Whangaparaoa, Auckland.

VIKING

Penguin Books (NZ) Ltd, cnr Rosedale and Airborne Roads, Albany, Auckland 1310, New Zealand

Penguin Books Ltd, 27 Wrights Lane, London W8 5TZ, England

Penguin USA, 375 Hudson Street, New York, NY 10014, United States

Penguin Books Australia Ltd, 487 Maroondah Highway, Ringwood, Australia 3134

Penguin Books Canada Ltd, 10 Alcorn Avenue, Toronto, Ontario, Canada M4V 3B2

Penguin Books Ltd, Registered Offices: Harmondsworth, Middlesex, England

First published in Penguin Books 1997

10 9 8 7 6 5 4 3 2

ISBN 0 670 87838 3

CONTENTS

FOREWORD

THE VAST MAJORITY of our European ancestors were not given to the culinary arts. They were conservative, middle and working class English stock who came to New Zealand to better their lives. They did not come to make a fuss! Ergo – food was fuel not fun. Maori had their own remarkable gardens and New Zealand, a country with a small population, was rich in food resources. All in all we had nothing to worry about. Nor did we need to extend ourselves. It was enough that there were meat and three vegies on the table. Downplaying emotion, colour, humour and individuality, we Kiwis took it upon ourselves to make consistency in everything a virtue. Including our eating habits. Thank heavens those days are long gone. *Simply New Zealand* is entertaining proof that in our own unique culinary corner of the world, we can compete with the best. Food is fun not fuel. And fun is here to stay!

Gary McCormick

INTRODUCTION

GREAT FOOD! Stunning scenery! A refrain I constantly hear from overseas writers, reviewers and visitors. So we decided to publish an up-to-date cookbook/travel guide offering a wide selection of the country's best dishes discovered on a region-by-region culinary journey that ranged from the major cities to the most remote locations.

We were delighted with the reception that we received from restaurants, brasseries and cafés throughout the country. Owners and chefs were extremely obliging and helpful. We thank them sincerely for their valued contributions to *Simply New Zealand.*

In travelling around the country, we discovered that while certain local specialties are still popular (such as whitebait on the West Coast or lamb in Canterbury), we found that chefs are enthusiastic in their use of foods from other regions. (North Island restaurants may feature salmon farmed in the South Island or Bluff oysters as well as locally sourced meats, vegetables or seafood.) And the best chefs, both new and experienced, are ready to experiment with new varieties of fruits and vegetables, many of which are produced here. This results in food combinations that are deliciously unique.

Jan Bilton, our Food Editor, has adapted these chef-created recipes to ensure they are easy to follow and prepare. Her task was not an easy one, since many creative chefs prepare their recipes from memory and do not write them down!

Combining some of the most creative cooking in the country with magnificent scenic photography from Ian Baker and other contributors, *Simply New Zealand* is simply a little bit different — both a cook's travel guide and a traveller's cookbook.

Bon voyage and bon appetit!

The photographs on the previous pages are: (2-3) Pohutukawas, (4-5) Marlborough Sounds, (6-7) Martinborough. The map on the facing page is a regional guide to our culinary journey.

Cliff Josephs
Publisher

NORTHLAND & AUCKLAND

Cape Maria van Diemen

Waitangi • Bay of Islands

• Whangarei

Kaipara Harbour
Whangaparaoa Peninsula
Muriwai •
Waitemata Harbour •
Auckland •
Manukau Harbour •
Port Waikato •

Hauraki Gulf • • Port Jackson
• Waiheke Island
• Coromandel
• Firth of Thames
Thames • • Pauanui Beach
• Waihi

COROMANDEL, BAY OF PLENTY & EAST CAPE

Bay of Plenty
Tauranga • • Mt. Maunganui
Raglan • • Hamilton • Te Puke
• Cambridge
• Rotorua

• East Cape

TARANAKI, KING COUNTRY & WAIKATO

Waitomo Caves •
Te Kuiti •

• Taupo
Lake Taupo
Tongariro National Park
• Mt. Tongariro
New Plymouth • Mt. Ngauruhoe
Cape Egmont • Mt. Taranaki Mt. Ruapehu
Hawke Bay
Napier •
Hastings • • Cape Kidnappers

Palmerston North •

WAIRARAPA & HAWKE'S BAY

MANAWATU & WELLINGTON

Tararua Range

Farewell Spit •
• Golden Bay
Abel Tasman National Park D'Urville Island • Te Horo
Tasman Bay • Waikanae • • Masterton
Karamea • Motueka • Wellington • • Martinborough
Nelson • Havelock • Lake Wairarapa
Murchison • Blenheim • Cloudy Bay Rimutakas
Nelson Lakes National Park • Cape Palliser
Westport •
Cook Strait

MARLBOROUGH & NELSON

Punakaiki •
Kaikoura Range
WEST COAST
Greymouth • • Kaikoura

Hokitika •

KAIKOURA & CANTERBURY

Southern Alps

Westland National Park
Franz Josef Glacier •
Fox Glacier •
Lake Paringa • • Mt. Cook
Haast • Canterbury Plains
• Haast Pass Ashburton •
Mt. Aspiring National Park

• Christchurch
Lyttelton • Lyttelton Harbour
• Akaroa
Banks Peninsula

CENTRAL OTAGO & FIORDLAND

• Timaru

Milford Sound Lake Wanaka
Mitre Peak • • Wanaka
Lake Wakatipu
Fiordland • Arrowtown • Oamaru
National Park Queenstown • • Clyde
Lake Te Anau • The Remarkables
Lake Manapouri •

• Otago Peninsula
• Dunedin

Gore • The • Balclutha
Catlins
Invercargill • • Owaka
Foveaux Strait • Bluff
Toetoes Bay

OTAGO & SOUTHLAND

• Stewart Island

NORTHLAND & AUCKLAND

FROM PORT WAIKATO TO CAPE MARIA VAN DIEMEN (pictured here), Northland has been scooped out into great bays and harbours like the Bay of Islands, Whangarei and Hokianga Harbours and the largest harbour in New Zealand, the Kaipara. Surrounding Auckland are the Manukau and Waitemata Harbours, and to the east is the Firth of Thames. Our first stop was the Bay of Islands, where the weather is subtropical and the deep sea fishing first class, with marlin, tuna, kingfish and shark to be won. One of our recipes highlights this prized catch: seared game fish with a salad of ripe juicy tomatoes and quail eggs. Further south we visited the Whangaparaoa Peninsula, which juts into the Hauraki Gulf, and found other eating delights such as a creamy pineapple sable with chocolate mousse. The Gulf is home to everything marine - from great container ships and holiday cruise ships to fully-appointed yachts and commercial fishing boats as well as to windsurfers, waterskiers and sports fishermen. Auckland is located on the southwest side of the Hauraki Gulf, and is now New Zealand's largest urban centre. A city of sails, commerce, and miles of beaches, Auckland offers a happy mix of city amenities, suburban malls, outdoor sports and fine restaurants. In Auckland we found fresh John Dory fillets nested on a salad with honey and lime undertones and steamed mussels spiced with a Thai curry sauce. This is the tasty beginning of our culinary journey.

CHARGRILLED SMOKED VENISON SAUSAGE ON BAKED AUBERGINE WITH BLACKBERRY PICKLE & PEPPERED BRIE

BLACKBERRY PICKLE
1 small jar port wine jelly
200 ml each raspberry vinegar, red wine vinegar
2 tablespoons brown sugar
1 cinnamon stick
2 bay leaves
3 cloves
200 ml red wine
500 g fresh or frozen blackberries

BAKED AUBERGINE
½ eggplant, sliced, salted and dried
butter
3 smoked venison sausages (from any good deli)
few slices Kapiti Peppered Brie cheese

To make the pickle, combine all ingredients except the blackberries in a saucepan and simmer for 5 minutes. Add blackberries and allow to cool. Makes enough for 8 servings. Bake eggplant in oven with a little butter. Chargrill venison sausage in griddle pan (or bake in oven). Arrange eggplant on plate, then venison sausage, then peppered brie. Finish with blackberry pickle and garnish with fresh garden herbs. Serves 1.

BISTRO 40, PAIHIA, BAY OF ISLANDS.

Preceding pages (14 & 15): Rawhiti Headlands, Bay of Islands. Rawhiti sits on the arm of Cape Brett, the lower part of the Bay of Islands, and looks across to the Kerikeri Inlet, the Purerua Peninsula and at inner bay islands such as Motukiekie, Urupukapuka and Waewaetoria. Urupukapuka in Otehei Bay is a sheltered island close to deep sea fishing zones and features an archaeological walk as well as marine life viewing from the Nautilus, a semi-submersible vessel.

WHERE TWO CULTURES MET

Below left is a vigorous carving from the Carrington Marae, Waitangi. Below: A waka at rest in the waters off Waitangi. Waitangi is best known as the place where in 1840 an agreement was signed between many Maori leaders and the British Crown. On the grounds of

the Treaty House, a Georgian-style edifice with part of its timber imported from Sydney, stands a meeting house or whare runanga. This meeting house is unique in having carvings provided by many different North Island tribes. Waitangi was one of New Zealand's earliest European settlements and Russell, which is near Waitangi and Paihia, was the first European town.

WARM SALAD OF SEARED GAME FISH WITH TOMATOES, QUAIL EGGS & POTATO

DRESSING

2 teaspoons cider vinegar
¼ cup olive oil
small bunch fresh basil
seasoning

SALAD

mixture of fancy lettuces
1 medium-sized potato,
scrubbed and boiled
2 tomatoes
8 quail eggs, boiled and peeled
8-10 capers
1 cucumber, sliced
2-3 slices each, red, green,
yellow capsicums

FISH

200 g game fish (tuna, swordfish, etc.)
100 ml soy sauce

To prepare dressing, blend all ingredients well. Arrange salad in a large bowl with sliced potatoes, tomatoes, quail eggs, capers, cucumber and capsicums. Slice game fish into 1 cm thick pieces and soak in soy sauce. Sear fish in smoking hot pan with a little olive oil until just underdone. Arrange fish in salad and drizzle dressing on the top.
Serves 1.

BISTRO 40, PAIHIA,
BAY OF ISLANDS.

PACIFIC HALF-SHELL OYSTERS TOPPED WITH MELON SALSA

MELON SALSA
¼ rock melon, finely diced
1 red chilli, seeded and finely diced
1 small red capsicum, finely diced
1 teaspoon chopped coriander
½ teaspoon Rose's Lime Juice
½ teaspoon fresh lime juice

OYSTERS
24 oysters in half shells
black pepper
shaved ice
rock salt
dried seaweed
2 limes to garnish
2 soft flour tortillas

To prepare melon salsa, combine rock melon, chilli, capsicum, coriander and lime juices in bowl. Allow flavours to mix for 30 minutes. Adjust seasoning, adding more lime juice if needed. Loosen oysters from shells. Season with black pepper. Top each oyster with ½ teaspoon melon salsa. On individual plates, scatter shaved ice and sprinkle with rock salt to stop ice melting. Scatter seaweed pieces on top of ice and salt and arrange 6 oysters in shells over the top. Garnish with lime wedges or twists and tortillas cut in wedges and deep fried. Serves 4.

STANMORE COTTAGE RESTAURANT, WHANGAPARAOA.

Islands in the Hauraki Gulf

PINEAPPLE SABLE WITH CHOCOLATE MOUSSE

SABLE

200 g butter
100 g caster sugar
2 eggs
zest of 1 lemon, 1 orange
3 drops vanilla essence
2 cups flour, sifted

Cream butter and sugar. Slowly add eggs a little at a time. Add zest and vanilla and fold in flour. Place in a container and refrigerate for 30 minutes. Dust work surface with flour and roll out dough. Using a cutter cut a large circle and place on a tray. Mark a centre line through diameter. When cold it will snap in half. Bake 180°C for 5-8 minutes until light in colour. Place on rack to cool. Store in an air-tight container.

CHOCOLATE MOUSSE

250 g chocolate
3 egg yolks
250 ml cream
2 egg whites
1 cup sugar
2 tablespoons rum

Melt chocolate in saucepan. Place egg yolks, cream and egg whites into separate bowls. Divide sugar evenly into each bowl. Add rum to egg yolks. Whip cream and refrigerate. Beat egg yolks until they form a stiff peak. Do the same with the egg whites. Fold chocolate into egg yolks. Fold in half the egg white, then add the cream. Lastly, fold in the remaining egg whites. Cover. Refrigerate overnight.

CANDIED PINEAPPLE

1 cup water

juice of 1 lemon

1 cup sugar

2 slices fresh pineapple cut 1 cm thick

**Combine water, lemon juice, sugar
and bring to the boil. Simmer. Cut
pineapple into even pieces. Place in
syrup. Cook until transparent. Leave
to cool. Add extra water if too thick,
or if mixture is reduced too quickly.**

RASPBERRY COULIS

1 cup sugar

2 cups water

2 tablespoons Grand Marnier

200 g raspberries

**Boil sugar and water until a light
syrup is formed. Add Grand Marnier
and raspberries and simmer. Blend
and strain through a fine sieve.**

ASSEMBLY

**To assemble, use a hot spoon and
spoon out mousse onto a plate.
Alternate mousse, sable, mousse
(as per photograph). Lastly, place
pineapple on top of sable. Dust with
icing sugar. Add coulis.
Serves 6.**

NAUTILUS RESTAURANT,
GULF HARBOUR VILLAGE,
WHANGAPARAOA.

*Following pages (22 & 23): Auckland City
skyline and Auckland's Waitemata Harbour
waterfront with the downtown commercial
and university areas and the new Sky Tower
Casino shown in the background.*

WHITE SAILS AND FOAMING WHITECAPS

On any bright and breezy weekend in Auckland, the sails are skimming over the harbour and to every corner of the Hauraki Gulf. Races to Kawau Island, leisurely jaunts to walks and picnics on Motutapu or Rangitoto Islands - the possibilities are nearly endless. The Whangaparaoa Peninsula and Tiritiri Matangi Island are also popular cruise destinations.

Nearly everybody in Auckland turned out to greet the America's Cup champions who brought the Auld Mug to New Zealand in 1996. The Hauraki Gulf is one of the training grounds where New Zealand yachties become expert in the art of sailing and learn respect for the power, surprises and thrills of the ever-changing wind and sea. And after a day's sailing, a relaxing dinner at the yacht club.

LEMON CHICKEN

2 cloves garlic, chopped
¼ teaspoon Chinese Five Spice
¼ cup cider vinegar
¼ cup lemon juice
zest of 1 lemon
¼ cup vegetable oil
1 whole chicken (No. 7)

Place all ingredients in a plastic bag large enough to hold the whole chicken. Place chicken in last. Seal bag and marinate for 24 hours. Remove chicken from bag and place on a wire rack on a tray. Roast at 180°C for 1 hour, basting occasionally with remainder of marinade. Cut and serve. Serves 4.

NAUTILUS RESTAURANT,
GULF HARBOUR VILLAGE,
WHANGAPARAOA.

CIN CIN
ORIENTAL-STYLE HOCKS

2 bacon or ham hocks
200 ml red wine
3 tablespoons soy sauce
2 each, cinnamon sticks, star anise
1 knob root ginger, sliced
3 cm piece orange peel
2 tablespoons palm sugar

Cover the hocks with water and boil for 30 minutes. Add all remaining ingredients and cook until tender, about 2 hours. Remove the hocks and reduce some of the liquid by three-quarters. Serve with boiled rice which has been moulded onto the serving plate. Spoon the sauce over the hocks. Can be accompanied by rocket leaves.
Serves 2.

CIN CIN ON
QUAY, AUCKLAND.

GULF ISLES

One can fly or float to Waiheke (it is about 35 minutes from Auckland by ferry), and its many beaches, leisurely lifestyle, resident artists, stylish cafés and vineyards have lured many Aucklanders to live there. There are also places to golf, mountain bike, bush walk and kayak. Other Gulf islands are Great Barrier, Little Barrier, Rakino and Kawau. Tiritiri Matangi Island is just off the end of the Whangaparaoa Peninsula and is now a bird refuge. Native bush is being restored, and excursions from Gulf Harbour regularly bring sightseers, who often help with organised plantings.

Matiata Bay, Waiheke Island. Waiheke is between Ponui Island and the Rangitoto, Motutapu and Rakino cluster of islands. The landward side of Waiheke Island looks across the Tamaki Strait to Maraetai and Beachlands. Its seaward side turns to the Coromandel.

SEARED JOHN DORY ON A WARM SALAD WITH A ROASTED RED CAPSICUM COULIS

ROASTED RED CAPSICUM COULIS

2 cups white wine
¼ cup white wine vinegar
2 bay leaves
6 black peppercorns
6 shallots, peeled, sliced
6 red capsicums, roasted, seeded, peeled
2 cups cream
sea salt to taste

SALAD

16 shallots
¾ cup virgin olive oil
24 French beans, blanched
4 large red capsicums, roasted, seeded,
peeled and cut into strips
20 cherry tomatoes
salt and pepper
¾ cup balsamic vinegar
1 tablespoon clear honey
juice of 2 limes

800 g John Dory fillets

To prepare the coulis, put white wine, white wine vinegar, bay leaves, peppercorns, shallots and capsicums into a heavy-bottomed pot and simmer until liquid is reduced. Then add cream, bring to boil, season with sea salt and blend to a fine red purée. To prepare the salad, sweat shallots off in half the olive oil. Add French beans, roasted capsicums and cherry tomatoes and season with salt and pepper. Add vinegar, honey and lime juice. Tip warm salad into a bowl and toss. Place warm salad in the centres of four hot plates, drizzle capsicum coulis around the outside of salads. To cook the fish, sear fillets in the remaining olive oil and place on top of warm salads.
Serves 4.

KERMADEC RESTAURANT,
AUCKLAND.

CHOCOLATE MARQUISE WITH ORANGE COMPOTE & SUMMER BERRIES

CHOCOLATE MARQUISE

325 g dark coverture chocolate
175 g butter
1 ¼ cups (about 8) egg whites
75 g sugar
100 ml whipped cream

COMPOTE

1 cup sugar
1 litre orange juice
3 tablespoons Grand Marnier
4 oranges, segments and zest

Line 8 plastic rings with silicon paper, reserve. Melt coverture and butter together. Whip egg white and sugar to soft peak and fold into chocolate and whipped cream mixture. Pipe the mix evenly into the plastic rings and refrigerate. To prepare the compote, caramelise the sugar, add the juice and reduce by half. Add the Grand Marnier, zest and orange segments. To assemble, pipe the chocolate across the plates, remove the marquise from the moulds and place in the centre of each plate. Fill one half with the orange compote and garnish with summer berries, tuilles and sugar sparkles. Serves 8.

ESSENCE, HERNE BAY,
AUCKLAND.

SESAME TOFU & SOBA STIR-FRY NOODLES

MARINADE

1½ cups shoyu
knob of ginger, finely chopped or grated
4 cloves garlic, finely diced
¼ cup water
¼ fresh chilli, finely diced

TOFU STIR FRY

¼ firm block of tofu, sliced
½ cup Arame seaweed
½ packet Soba noodles
sesame oil
mixture of green vegetables, eg julienned celery, cucumber, capsicum, spring onions, courgette, and shredded cabbage
handful of sesame seeds, toasted
juice and zest of ½ lemon

Combine marinade ingredients and cover sliced tofu. Leave for 2-4 hours. Meanwhile cover seaweed with water and soak until soft for 5-10 minutes. Drain. To prepare noodles, cook in boiling water until 'al denté' (soft but firm). Drain and rinse under cold water. Toss a little toasted sesame oil through to prevent sticking. Drain tofu but save marinade. Lightly toss in flour and fry in pan with a little sesame oil until crisp on both sides. Put to one side. Heat wok with 1-2 tablespoons sesame oil, add vegetables, seaweed, sesame seeds and noodles. Add half the marinade and stir-fry for 5-10 minutes. Serve on a bed of salad greens, garnish with sliced fried tofu and black sesame seeds. Add lemon juice and zest for a twist.

ATOMIC CAFÉ, PONSONBY, AUCKLAND.

STEAMED MUSSELS AND RED THAI CURRY SAUCE WITH COCONUT CREAM & CORIANDER

MIREPOIX

1 onion,
1 carrot,
1 celery stick,
1¼ leeks, finely diced

RED THAI CURRY SAUCE

1 tablespoon each, chopped garlic,
grated root ginger,
red curry paste
2 teaspoons tomato paste
2 cups fish stock
1 small can peeled tomatoes
½ can coconut cream
1 coriander root
sea salt and pepper

STEAMED MUSSELS

½ cup olive oil
32 medium mussels, cleaned
1¼ cups white wine
chopped coriander to garnish

To make the curry sauce, sweat off mirepoix with garlic and ginger, add curry paste and tomato paste and cook until soft and dry. Add fish stock, tomatoes, coconut cream, coriander and seasoning. Bring to the boil and cook for 20 minutes. Pass through a sieve. To prepare the mussels, heat oil in a heavy-bottomed pan. Add mussels and put lid on pot.

As mussels are just opening, add white wine and reduce. Add the curry sauce. Check seasoning and garnish with chopped coriander.
Serves 4.

KERMADEC RESTAURANT,
AUCKLAND.

SECLUSION CLOSE TO THE COSMOPOLITAN

Muriwai is about 40 km from downtown Auckland or less than 20 km from Kumeu. It has an unspoiled beach and boisterous, often dangerous surf, long rambling walks uphill and down dale and a wonderland of craggy cliffs, interesting tidepools and huge boulders carpeted with starfish, barnacles, mussels, and whelks.

Left: Flax plants fringe a lookout point over Muriwai Beach. One of Auckland's better known west coast surf beaches, it is north of Piha on the segment of coast between the entrances to Kaipara Harbour and Manukau Harbour. The iron-sand beach is long and level and bordered by low dunes. The spot is also a favourite of hang-gliding enthusiasts, who launch themselves from the Maori Bay cliffs.

Below: The gannet colony at Muriwai, where the nesting gannets and their chicks can be observed from a distance. This colony is one of the three known mainland nesting sites in New Zealand. The others are at Cape Kidnappers (south part of Hawke's Bay) and Farewell Spit (extreme north of the South Island).

COROMANDEL, BAY OF PLENTY & EAST CAPE

ON THESE PAGES IS A TYPICAL Coromandel Peninsula scene, with gentle sloping farmland, water views and rugged hills. Although the peninsula feels very secluded, it is only about an hour's drive from Auckland, and its attractions (including fishing for trevally, snapper and tarakihi) make it a favourite holiday spot. We began our journey in Thames and, after feasting on flounder in white wine sauce, drove north to the Tapu-Coroglen Road leading to Whitianga. South of Whitianga on the Coromandel east coast, we found superb recipes like upside-down-cake with toffee sauce. The Bay of Plenty was next, with its citrus, kiwifruit and tamarillo orchards. The 200-km-wide bay is rich in New Zealand history, Maori culture, natural resources and good food! In Tauranga we found a deliciously unusual licorice ice cream and discovered that White Island has geological links to Rotorua, the next stop on our itinerary. In Rotorua, showplace of one of the three most well-known geyser groups in the world, we found a sensationally scrumptious version of salmon fillets with mozzarella cheese and capsicum sauce. Then we toured the East Cape, home of rich farmland, remote beaches, mineral hot springs and beach reserves. We discovered many wonderful recipes in this varied and interesting region.

Tapu end of the Coroglen Road on the
Coromandel. If you drive north from
Thames to Tapu, you can cross the
Coromandel Peninsula to Coroglen.

BRIAN BORU FLOUNDER

WHITE WINE SAUCE
½ cup white wine
1 teaspoon lemon juice
½ cup cream
salt and pepper
pinch chicken stock powder
1 teaspoon chopped parsley
1 flounder

Mix together white wine, lemon juice
and cream and simmer until slightly
reduced. Add seasoning, stock and
parsley and reduce further, stirring
continually to dissolve the stock
powder.

Grill flounder on both sides. Cook
until white side turns golden brown.
Pour white wine sauce over flounder.
Serve with French fries and salad.
Serves 1.

BRIAN BORU HOTEL, THAMES.

*View at Whitianga wharf.
You can drive south from Whitianga via
Coroglen to Tairua Beach. A popular resort
town, Tairua has a spectacular harbour
from which you can see Shoe and
Slipper Islands. Just across the inlet from
Tairua is Pauanui Beach, where the lovely
Puka Park Lodge is situated. Secluded in
pristine bush, the lodge offers the finest
dining and accommodation.*

RHUBARB UPSIDE-DOWN CAKE WITH TOFFEE AND COCONUT MILK SAUCE

*400 g rhubarb stems
175 g butter, softened
150 g caster sugar
175 g self-raising flour
½ teaspoon baking powder
1 heaped tablespoon unblanched ground
almonds
1 teaspoon ground cinnamon
3 eggs, beaten*

**Cut the rhubarb stems into 5 mm
pieces and place into the bottom
of individual ramekins.
Cream butter and sugar until light
and pale in colour. Combine flour,
baking powder, almonds and
cinnamon. Fold into the creamed
mixture, alternating with the eggs.
The sponge should be fairly soft.
Drop spoonfuls over the fruit as
carefully as possible, trying not to
disturb it. Dip a soup spoon in cold
water and smooth the surface of the
cake flat. Bake in a moderate oven
180°C for 30-35 minutes. Allow to
cool in the moulds for a minute or
two then turn out.**

WELCOMING WHITIANGA

It is less than a 50 km coastline drive along Highway 25 from Tairua to Whitianga. A very accessible anchorage, Whitianga is a holiday resort with ferry links to Ferry's Landing and Flaxmill Bay. The outdoors minded will be delighted by the swimming at Buffalo Beach, the good scallop hunting, and the places to go fishing and yachting. A visitor can also choose to wind surf, golf, abseil or horse trek as well as try river rafting or rock hounding. There is also a Craft Trail, a Heritage Trail and the Purangi Winery and Craft Gallery. Whitianga is also the base for Air Coromandel.

TOFFEE AND COCONUT MILK SAUCE

250 g unsalted butter
250 g brown sugar
3 tablespoons Butterscotch Schnapps
800 ml coconut milk
200 ml cream

Melt the butter in a saucepan. When boiling, add brown sugar and let the two boil into each other. Add the Butterscotch Schnapps, then add in coconut milk and cream. Bring to the boil, simmer for 5 minutes, strain and pour over the upside-down cakes and serve with homemade vanilla bean ice cream.
Serves about 6.

SHELLS RESTAURANT & BAR,
TAIRUA BEACH.

BAKED SUPREME OF SOUTH ISLAND SALMON WRAPPED IN NORI, ON A BED OF GINGER-INFUSED VEGETABLES

VEGETABLES
1 tablespoon diced ginger
5 g dried seaweed
1 tablespoon water
1 each, small carrot and
courgette, finely diced
2 tablespoons skinned and diced
red capsicum
2 tablespoons sake
salt and freshly ground black pepper
1 tablespoon each fish sauce,
rice wine vinegar

SALMON PARCELS
4 x 200 g supremes
(fillets) of salmon
salt and pepper
lemon juice
4 sheets nori (dried seaweed)

To marinate the ginger-infused vegetables, blanch the ginger in plenty of boiling water for 15 minutes. Drain well. Soak the dried seaweed in the water for 1 hour then drain well and chop finely.

Mix all the remaining vegetable garnish ingredients together with seaweed and ginger.

Cover with plastic film and marinate for 24 hours in fridge. To wrap the salmon parcels, cut salmon fillets in half and season with salt, pepper and lemon juice. Fold over to create a square.

Brush with a little water to soften, place salmon in centre of each sheet of nori and wrap in a parcel Bake in oven at 180°C for 13 minutes. Place warmed vegetables loosely on centre of plate, slice baked salmon on an angle and place onto vegetables. Serves 6.

PUKA PARK LODGE RESTAURANT, PAUANUI BEACH.

VENISON MEDALLIONS WITH SUNDRIED TOMATO & STRAWBERRY CHUTNEY

200 g Venison Denver leg
1 tablespoon olive oil
¼ cup red wine
50 g sundried tomatoes
6 strawberries
1 tablespoon strawberry conserve
seasoning to taste

Slice venison into medallions across the grain.
Heat a heavy pan with olive oil until very hot. Fry venison for 1-2 minutes each side until cooked rare.
To make the sauce, reduce red wine to half the quantity. Add sliced sundried tomatoes and strawberries and thicken sauce with strawberry conserve. Serve with the venison. Serves 1.

Serve with a bottle of full-bodied red wine (suggestion: Villa Maria Merlot Syrah Cabernet).

KESSALLS RESTAURANT & BAR, PAUANUI.

LICORICE ICE CREAM WITH FRESHLY SQUEEZED ORANGE JUICE

1 litre milk
8 egg yolks
1 1/4 cups caster sugar
1 tablespoon Galliano
2 cups cream
1 kg softened licorice pieces
freshly squeezed orange juice
chocolate-coated dried oranges

Boil the milk. Beat egg yolks and sugar until thick. Add milk, return to a low heat, stirring constantly until thick enough to coat the back of a wooden spoon. Chill until cool, add Galliano, cream and licorice and churn in an ice cream maker or food processor until creamy. Serve in a glass with fresh orange juice and chocolate-coated dried oranges.

SOMERSET COTTAGE, TAURANGA.

Right, sunset over Matamata. West of Tauranga, rural Matamata has over 20 thoroughbred studs, many sheep and dairy farms and good access to trout fishing and Kaimai Range walking tracks.

SHELTERED ANCHORAGE

The protected Port of Tauranga bustles with commercial activity. The farmlands of Tauranga yield kiwifruit, tamarillo, feijoa and citrus crops, and its offshore waters yield the big game fish that attract sports fishermen to try their luck. The ocean near Mayor and Motiti Islands is especially good for anglers. Other attractions are the city's jazz festival, its many historical monuments and buildings from colonial times and the Tauranga Historic Village, which brings to life New Zealand's colonial era. Walks include Longridge and McLaren Falls Parks, the Puketoki Scenic Reserve, the Katikati Bird Gardens, the Waikareao Estuary and Ohauiti Walkways, and Rerekawau Falls. Many spas and pools can be enjoyed, including the salt water pools at Mt Maunganui, the Maketu, Welcome Bay, and Katikati hot pools and the Plummer's Point Sapphire Hot Springs. A kiwifruit theme park called Kiwi Country specialises in showing the visitor every aspect of kiwifruit production and export.

FRESH CHICKEN LIVERS WITH FIG TAPENADE & RASPBERRY VINEGAR

FIG TAPENADE
¼ cup chopped figs
2 tablespoons brandy
¼ cup each water, pitted olives, olive oil
3 anchovy fillets
salt and pepper
1 tablespoon each capers, lemon juice,
balsamic vinegar
1 teaspoon Dijon mustard

POTATO RÖSTI
1 large potato, washed
2 tablespoons oil
extra oil
16 fresh chicken livers
flour
2 tablespoons clarified butter
½ onion, sliced
2 tablespoons each Marsala,
raspberry vinegar
4 teaspoons fig tapenade
4 small potato rösti

To make the fig tapenade, simmer figs, brandy and water for 5 minutes, add remaining ingredients and process until smooth. To make the potato rösti, slice potato into fine julienne and mix with oil. Fry four moulded round shapes in oil. When brown, turn over and fry until crisp. Drain on absorbent paper. To prepare chicken livers, flour livers in a sieve, shake off any excess flour. Melt clarified butter in a frying pan and add livers.

A TAURANGA TREK

Another lovely vacation area is shown above in the photo taken from the top of Mt Maunganui looking out over the coastal town of Mt Maunganui and its ocean surf beaches. Here, holidaymakers will find both hot and saltwater pools plus good swimming and water sports near the steep mountain cone that rises from the beach at one end of the peninsula. From the summit there are splendid views of offshore islands and Tauranga, which is linked to Mt Maunganui by the harbour bridge. Near the mountain are the docks for the Port of Tauranga. The area is also close to Te Puke and is a short drive to Rotorua, famed for its geysers, hot springs, blue-green lakes and other natural wonders.

Cook on high heat until brown on both sides (be careful as they can spit). Add onion, then Marsala. Place onto plate. Return pan to heat, deglaze with raspberry vinegar, then pour around livers. Garnish with potato rösti and fig tapenade. Serves 4.

SOMERSET COTTAGE, TAURANGA.

FILLETS OF SALMON WITH MOZZARELLA, BASIL & CAPSICUM ON A LIME SAUCE

800 g salmon fillet, skinned, filleted and
with all bones removed, including
pin bones
½ medium-sized red capsicum, thinly
sliced and lightly fried in olive oil
4 basil leaves
½ cup mozzarella

POACHING LIQUOR AND SAUCE

½ cup finely diced onion
zest and juice of 4 limes
¾ cup dry white wine
pinch freshly ground black pepper
and salt
1 cup cream
50 g butter

To prepare salmon fillets, cut salmon into eight equal squares. Take four squares and place the capsicum, a basil leaf and mozzarella on top of each, then cover with four remaining pieces of salmon. Hold together with a toothpick, then sprinkle with freshly ground black pepper and a pinch of salt. To cook salmon, take a large stainless steel or Teflon-coated frypan (large enough to accommodate the salmon) and place onion, lime zest and dry wine in the pan. Place the salmon fillets in the pan, cover with a lid, and gently steam the fish for about 7-8 minutes or until just cooked. Do not dry the fish. Remove the fish from the pan, place on a dish and cover with foil and keep warm.

To make the sauce, reduce cooking liquor by two-thirds over a high heat. Add cream and lime juice, pinch of black pepper and salt and reduce by half (still on a fierce heat). Remove from the heat and whisk in 50 g of butter. Do not melt the butter first. Season to taste.

To serve the salmon, place on a plate and drizzle the sauce around. Can be served with your favourite salad and vegetables. Complement with small poached potatoes. It is also delightful served on lightly steamed courgettes cut spaghetti style.

Serves 4.

RUMOURS, ROTORUA.

RACK OF LAMB WITH TARRAGON SAUCE & KUMARA CAKE

1 large kumara
4 racks of lamb (French racked, chined and silverskin removed)
½ cup chopped fresh tarragon, mint and parsley
black pepper and salt

SAUCE

1 tablespoon each finely diced onion, dry tarragon, tarragon vinegar
½ cup dry red wine
1 cup demi glaze (packet-made brown sauce will substitute well in a home situation)
25 g butter

Microwave kumara on high until cooked, remove flesh, place through a mincer or food processor and fashion into 4 quite thick cakes. Pan fry in clarified butter and set aside. Coat the lamb racks in the herb mix (outer surface only). Season with black pepper and salt. Heat a thick-bottomed pan, then seal the lamb rack until a nice brown colour is achieved on both sides. Place in a medium oven and cook to the degree you prefer. Do not dry out meat - about 15 minutes should produce a medium-cooked rack. To make the sauce, place onion, tarragon, tarragon vinegar and wine in a small saucepan and reduce by two-thirds. Add in brown sauce, bring to boil.

Remove from heat and whip in the butter. (Do not heat further). To serve, pour sauce onto centre of four plates. Place kumara cake in the middle of each plate. Cut racks into individual pieces by slicing between the bones and lay neatly around the kumara cake. Serve with your choice of vegetables.
Serves 4.

RUMOURS, ROTORUA.

Far left: An impressive carving from Rotorua. The city and environs have a wealth of living Maori culture: from ethnic exhibits and craft studios to the way of life of Rotorua's Maori residents. Maori dance, music, weaving, cooking and carving plus other activities can be enjoyed.

Left: Silica formations at Rotorua. Much of the Rotorua area was reshaped by the violent 1886 explosion of Mt Tarawera, which destroyed existing formations such as the often-painted Pink and White Terraces. But visitors can still see silica terraces, hillocks and naturally shaped sculpture, much of which is coloured by the algae that flourish in the steaming, mineralised waters.

Right: A beach on the East Cape near Gisborne.

Below: A caravan sits in a secluded glen in Tokomaru Bay. Situated about 92 km from Gisborne on East Cape Road (Highway 35), Tokomaru Bay is one of the fine beaches to be seen along the road from Gisborne to Opotiki.

TARANAKI, KING COUNTRY & WAIKATO

FROM THE AIR CAPE EGMONT dominates the Taranaki region. Pictured on these two pages is snow-capped Mount Taranaki, which is situated in the very centre of Cape Egmont and is encircled by lush dairy and sheep pasture. This rich pasturage fostered the establishment of cheesemakers who were first famed for their tangy cheddar cheese. Now local cheesemakers are building on that success by producing many types of cheeses for the domestic market and for export. We began our travels east of Mount Taranaki in the Tongariro National Park area. From there we bring you a very special pumpkin recipe. Then we drove south to Lake Taupo, the largest freshwater lake in the Southern Hemisphere, and sampled a bold onion frittata garnished with black olive pesto. After that we travelled through the lush rolling hillsides of the King Country, which still contains untouched forests and pristine rivers like the Waipa, Mokau and Awakino. (In this book, the King Country encompasses the North Island Central Plateau, Lake Taupo and Waikato.) We ended our pleasant stay in the lovely Waikato environs, where we sampled a scallop platter rich with garlic taste and salmon fillets bathed in a wine, whisky and butter sauce. The tempting dishes from this lush and dramatic region are both unique and memorable.

54

Right: This August 1995 photo of Mount Ruapehu captures the awe-inspiring billows of ash and steam that poured from its depths, closing ski fields but drawing throngs of volcano watchers. The eruptions caused great hardship to the North Island's most popular winter sports playground, which includes the Whakapapa ski fields, the Chateau, the golf course and the camping areas.

Inset: Mount Ngauruhoe rising above the Rangipo Desert in Tongariro National Park. This spectacular area, which lies between Turangi in the north and Waiouru and Okahune in the south, was given in trust to the Tuwharetoa tribe so that it might be preserved for our generation and future generations to come. Ngauruhoe's base is entwined with its close northern neighbour, Mount Tongariro.

MUMU PUMPKIN

4 miniature pumpkins
2 bananas, sliced
100 g thinly sliced fresh pineapple
2 shallots, finely chopped
orange-scented olive oil
1 clove garlic, peeled and sliced
1 similarly sized piece of ginger root,
peeled and sliced
400 ml coconut cream
salt and pepper

Blanch and peel pumpkins, remove
seeds and fill with banana and
pineapple. Place in casserole dish.
Sweat shallots in a little
orange-scented olive oil, add sliced
garlic and ginger, add coconut cream,
salt and pepper, and simmer for 10
minutes. Strain over pumpkins,
cover and bake until tender.
Remove pumpkins, reduce sauce,
adjust seasoning and consistency
and pour around the pumpkins.
Good served with pork, poultry,
lamb or beef.
Serves 4.

THE RUAPEHU ROOM,
THE GRAND CHATEAU,
TONGARIRO NATIONAL PARK.

Waiting for the first visitors... All alone in the dawn, a wooden bench sits before Lake Taupo, the largest freshwater lake in the Southern Hemisphere. Its stillness does not reveal that nearly 2000 years ago a volcanic eruption took place here, with ash and pumice hurled more than 100 km away.

LAKESIDE HOLIDAYS

Lake Taupo graces the centre of the North Island and is on a northeast line from Mount Ruapehu, Ngauruhoe, Tongariro and Pihanga - and is just north of Turangi. The lake is about 619 sq km in area and about 25 km long. The town of Taupo looks southwest over Acacia Bay and across the lake, whose northern rim is bitten out by several other deep coves. The Taupo area is a wonderland for those on a holiday - with thermal baths and pools, jet boating and water skiing and many walks nearby. The Waitahanui River is just one of many good fishing spots where fat and feisty trout can be taken.

FILLED FARMHOUSE LOAVES

There are more varieties of fillings than there are farmhouse loaves. At Replete there is no official recipe for this dish, except it uses the freshest of ingredients and tasty flavour combinations.

1 olive, walnut or rye loaf
spicy mango or your favourite chutney
cottage cheese
Mesclun salad mix
ham or pastrami
alfalfa sprouts

Cut one end off the loaf, being sure not to remove too much. Hollow out the loaf, leaving a thin layer of soft bread under the crust. Keep the scooped-out bread for stuffings, etc. Spread the inside of the cavity with the chutney, then fill the loaf with the variety of fillings starting with the cottage cheese. Pack the fillings in as tightly as you can so they hold their place once the loaf is sliced. Pack in the layer of salad mix, then compress it down with the ham, holding everything in place with your free hand. Fill the remaining cavity with the sprouts. To serve, slice the loaf into thick servings, then carefully place onto a plate. Serve with tossed salad, pasta salad and, if you're really hungry, smoked salmon-filled bagels. Makes one standard loaf.

REPLETE FOOD COMPANY, CAFÉ/DELI & CATERING CONSULTANCY, TAUPO.

ONION FRITTATA WITH BLACK OLIVE PESTO

This dish is very much in keeping with Italian brasserie-style food. It is light, quick, easy to prepare and is based around what is in season. The dish can be increased in size to be a complete entrée or reduced in portion size to become an antipasto.

FRITTATA

7 x no. 6 eggs
1/2 cup grated fresh Parmesan
freshly-ground black pepper and
Maldon crystal salt
extra-virgin olive oil
1 medium-sized red onion, sliced

BLACK OLIVE PESTO

250 g black olives, in brine (stoned weight)
1 tablespoon capers
1 small clove garlic
zest of 1/2 lemon
enough extra-virgin olive oil to make a firm paste
freshly ground black pepper and Maldon crystal salt

TOSSED SALAD

enough Mesclun salad mix for 6 servings (allow approximately 35-40 g per portion)
olive oil
freshly ground black pepper and Maldon crystal salt

Beat the eggs in a large bowl. Mix in the cheese and season to taste. Heat the frypan over a steady flame with a little olive oil (suggest you use a 25 cm frypan). Add in the sliced onion and cook until tender.

NATIVE PARROTS AND ANCIENT TREES

Not far east of Lake Taupo is the Whirinaki Forest, part of which is rooted in the deep ash and pumice laid down by the Lake Taupo eruption. This forest, known worldwide for its ancient podocarp trees, was declared a DOC conservation park in 1984; thus preserving its rimu, totara, matai, miro and kahikatea from further logging. These coniferous trees are related to the yew family and are home to kakas, large native parrots which love podocarp fruit, honeydew from beech trees, insects from rotting wood and sap both from tawa and the imported pine that grows next to the forest. Sadly, because much of the Whirinaki Forest was so heavily logged, the kakas are under threat because of limited habitat and predators.

Increase the heat and add in the egg mix. Cook until golden on one side. Lift the edges of the frittata as it cooks, then turn and cook until golden on the remaining side. Turn out onto a clean plate and allow to cool completely. Set aside.

To make the pesto, drain and dry the olives and capers. Stone the olives, then place them in a food processor with the capers, garlic and zest. Blend to a medium-fine texture, adding in the olive oil as you go to form a firm paste. Remove from the blender and place in a clean bowl. Season to taste. Set aside.

To serve, cut the frittata into small even wedges and arrange three on each plate. Spoon a little pesto evenly on each one. Very lightly toss the Mesclun in olive oil, then place a portion in the centre of each plate. Grind over plenty of pepper and sprinkle with a few whole Maldon salt crystals. Serve with a dry Italian-style white wine.

Serves 6.

REPLETE CAFÉ/DELI & CATERING CONSULTANCY, TAUPO.

Screened by a green veil of leaves as the sun sets, a homeward-bound yacht catches the late evening breezes on Lake Taupo.

Right: Waitomo Caves near Te Kuiti. Visitors to these world-famous caverns can ride boats through the Glow-worm Grotto, hauntingly illuminated in alluring light given off by the larvae of tiny gnats. Sports lovers can try abseiling and ladder climbing, water rafting or black water rafting to explore other parts of the caves.

Below: Surfers at Raglan Beach watch the waves. The surf is not the only attraction in this easily reached resort area about an hour's drive west from Hamilton. There is good fishing and whitebaiting in and around the rivers and harbour, and Pirongia Forest Park is not far away. The park's two main tracks, the Wairake and Te Toki, offer scenic walks up Mount Karioi and Mount Pirongia. On the road to Kawhia is another walk - to lovely Bridal Veil Falls.

WAITOMO CAVES

Waitomo – The place where the waters of the Waitomo River plunge suddenly into a hillside. The caves are numerous and connected, with most of the tunnels still unexplored. About twelve million years ago, the Waitomo Caves began to form as water dissolved limestone and redeposited it inside the network of caverns. This process creates downward-pointing stalagtites, and upward-pointing stalagmites as well as wrinkles, curls and other fantastic shapes in limestone.

Inside the best known part, Glow-worm Grotto, the larval stage of a gnat spins slender, crystal-clear fishing lines to trap other insects for dinner. The chemical lights in the worms can be flicked on and off as they choose, bathing the fantasia of threads that look like micro-waterfalls hanging hazily in the grotto. A specialist museum at the caves explains in full detail about the geology and history of the area as well as the living ecosystem and the fossils found there.

64

SAUCE

1 nip whisky
1 teaspoon dill
1 tablespoon sparkling wine
25 g butter

SALMON

2 x 100 g fillets salmon, skin on
salt and freshly ground
black pepper to taste
flour
50 g vegetables, julienned and blanched
1 lemon slice and sprig of fresh fennel
to garnish

To make sauce, mix together all ingredients and simmer until blended. Roll salmon in seasoned flour and place on a grill in an oven dish. Oven bake at 200°C until cooked and arrange on a bed of julienned vegetables. Cover with the sauce and garnish with a slice of lemon and some fennel.
Serves 1.

LEFT BANK INTERNATIONAL RESTAURANT & BAR, HAMILTON, WAIKATO.

CHARRED TUNA LOIN WITH WILTED SPINACH AND LIME & GRAPEFRUIT BEURRE BLANC

MIXED TOMATO SALAD

100 g cherry tomatoes
50 g each, sundried tomatoes, shallots,
chives
3 cloves garlic
3 tablespoons each, balsamic vinegar,
sundried tomato oil

BEURRE BLANC

100 ml each, lime juice, grapefruit juice
100 g shallots
1 teaspoon peppercorns
1 bay leaf
200 g butter

TUNA

160 g tuna steak
salt and pepper
1 teaspoon grated lemon rind
100 g spinach leaves

To make the salad, quarter the tomatoes, chop the sundried tomatoes, shallots, chives and garlic and combine with vinegar and oil. To make the beurre blanc, reduce the liquids and flavourings by half, strain, then slowly add cold butter without boiling the mixture. Sprinkle the tuna with salt, pepper and lemon rind. Chargrill for about 2 minutes each side. Sauté spinach in a saucepan for about 1 minute. Serve the tuna on the spinach topped with the beurre blanc and the tomato salad on the side. Serves 1.

RUSTICI BRASSERIE, HAMILTON, WAIKATO

PICASSO'S SCALLOP PLATTER

1 teaspoon each, chopped root
ginger, crushed garlic, butter
5 scallops
salt and pepper
2 teaspoons each, cheese sauce, raspberry
purée, apricot purée, sesame sauce,
cardamom sauce, blueberry purée*
½ cup boiled rice
15 g julienned vegetables
1 puff pastry leaf
1 fennel sprig
cracked pepper

*Note: You may use a combination
of your favourite sauces.

Sauté ginger and garlic in butter, add scallops and seasoning.

Prepare all sauces separately. Boil the rice, prepare the julienned vegetables and make the leaf with puff pastry. Centre the rice on a small dish and arrange the six sauces around it in equal amounts with colours alternating. Arrange the scallops on the rice and garnish with the vegetables and pastry leaf and top with a sprig of fennel. Add cracked pepper around the plate and serve. Serves 1.

LEFT BANK INTERNATIONAL
RESTAURANT & BAR,
HAMILTON, WAIKATO.

Preceding pages (66 & 67): Sheep graze in a lush and peaceful Waikato setting near Cambridge - about two hours south of Auckland.

Left: The mighty Waikato, slow and serene. Born from Lake Taupo, the Waikato travels north more than 400 km to meet the Tasman Sea south of Manukau Harbour.

WAIRARAPA & HAWKE'S BAY

THIS PLEASANT FARMING REGION is on the road to Cape Palliser. At the extreme southern end of the North Island, Cape Palliser is not far south of Martinborough, where we began our good food search in the Wairarapa. Martinborough, which has gained international status as a fine-wine producer, is situated east of Lake Wairarapa and it shares the related pursuits of farming and market gardening with communities such as Carterton, Greytown and Eketahuna, which perches above the Makakahi River Gorges. In Martinborough we dined on tender beef eye fillet dressed with well-seasoned jus and found a salmon terrine whose taste was spectacular. Then we drove north to fast-growing Masterton, where we found a chewy-good crostata garnished with fresh rosemary. Continuing north to Hawke's Bay, we basked in the sunshine that fosters the region's agricultural success. Abundant grapes, fruits and vegetables feed into local food processing companies, wineries and food exporting companies. Napier and Hastings restaurants contributed excellent recipes, such as a mouth-watering fresh-fruit terrine and a lemon-herbed lamb roulade stuffed with aubergine. One of the brightest stars in the Hawke's Bay area is viniculture, whose success is garnering international respect and financial rewards. You'll love both the wines and the recipes of this region!

TERRINE OF SALMON
AND CABBAGE

1 savoy or green cabbage
150 g smoked salmon
450 g fresh salmon
salt and white pepper

Blanch cabbage leaves, refresh in iced
water, dry in a tea towel or salad
spinner. Line a 650 ml capacity terrine
mould with plastic film (oil mould to
help plastic film stick). Allow film to
overlap for folding over the top. Line
mould with cabbage leaves, allowing
enough overlap to fold over the top.
Line cabbage with smoked salmon,
allowing overlap to fold over the top.
Layer 3-4 layers of salmon with
cabbage, packing well and seasoning
well with salt and pepper. Finish by
folding the overlapping cabbage and
salmon over the top, adding more if
necessary. Fold gladwrap over to
cover. Cook, covered and well sealed
with foil, in a deep waterbath at 180°C
for 25-30 minutes. Test with a metal
skewer - it should be hot when
removed. Remove immediately, press
with weights (2 tins of canned food).
Cool and refrigerate. To serve, slice
and steam or microwave until just
warm. Accompany with a soy
flavoured Beurre Blanc or a classic
Beurre Blanc spiked with a little caviar
or lumpfish roe (rinsed and added at
the last minute). A soy vinaigrette or
mayonnaise is a simpler
accompaniment.
Serves 8.

AYLSTONE, PRIVATE
LODGINGS, WINE LIBRARY &
LARDER, MARTINBOROUGH.

GRILLED BEEF EYE FILLET WITH OVEN ROASTED TOMATOES, WILTED ROCKET, WARERCRESS & BEEF JUS

2 tomatoes
salt and ground black pepper
olive oil
rocket and watercress leaves
melted butter
BEEF JUS
300 ml beef stock
¼ teaspoon tomato paste
¼ cup Winslow Cabernet
Sauvignon/Franc

1 beef eye fillet steak per serve

Slice tomatoes in half and lightly season. Drizzle with olive oil and place on an oven tray cut side up. Dry slowly in 150°C oven for approximately 3 hours. Rinse and pat dry the rocket and watercress leaves. Toss in a little olive oil and melted butter. To make the beef jus, heat stock, tomato paste and wine until reduced to a quarter of the original volume. Season and tie to shape a piece of eye fillet for each serving. Grill 3 minutes each side or as required. Assemble on warm plate with other ingredients.
Serves 1.

THE MARTINBOROUGH BISTROT,
MARTINBOROUGH HOTEL,
MARTINBOROUGH.

*Left: Seals at part of Cape Palliser's
rugged coastline.*

RED CAPSICUM PESTO TARTLET ON A BED OF MARINATED AUBERGINE SLICES WITH LEMON BASIL DRESSING

Prepare and bake some small tartlet cases from your favourite savoury shortcrust recipe.

AUBERGINE (EGGPLANT)

1 eggplant

salt

basil and mint

1 clove garlic, peeled and sliced

cracked pepper

olive oil

RED CAPSICUM PESTO

4 red capsicums

¼ cup pine nuts

1 clove of garlic, chopped

salt and pepper

a little grated Parmesan cheese

¼ cup olive oil

CUSTARD

2 tablespoons pesto

1 egg

¼ cup cream

DRESSING

handful of lemon basil

1 cup olive oil

2 teaspoons lemon juice

salt and black pepper

To prepare the eggplant, peel, slice and sprinkle with salt. Leave to sweat out the moisture. Rinse and dry. Layer with basil, mint, garlic and cracked pepper. Add olive oil and compress layers to remove air bubbles, make sure it is completely covered. Cover and refrigerate. To prepare the pesto, roast, peel and de-seed capsicum.

CASTLEPOINT AND WINERY CASKS

The photo above shows the lighthouse at Castlepoint, which is on the coast about 68 km due east of Masterton. Castlepoint is the site of an annual horse race on the dunes, and there are many other activities to enjoy

Blend in a food processor with pine nuts, garlic, salt and pepper, Parmesan cheese and drizzle in the olive oil. To prepare the custard, beat pesto with egg and cream. Pour into two tartlet cases. Bake until set in a moderate oven. Multiply the recipe if more tartlets are required. To make the dressing, chop the basil and add to warm olive oil. Leave to infuse. Before serving, whisk in the lemon juice, salt and black pepper. Serve the tartlets with eggplant and dressing. Makes 2 tartlets but enough pesto dressing and eggplant for 6 or more servings.

THE MARTINBOROUGH BISTROT, MARTINBOROUGH HOTEL, MARTINBOROUGH.

as well such as swimming, surf casting, reef fishing and floundering. About 50 km from Masterton is Martinborough, which hosts a yearly wine festival. Visitors can taste wines from local boutique wineries and visit arts and crafts stalls where local artists display their work.

CRISPY COUNTRY
CROSTATA

CRUST

1 cup chilled flour
125 g chilled butter
4 tablespoons sour cream
1 tablespoon lemon juice
¼ cup iced water
¼ cup coarse cornmeal

FILLING

2 tablespoons olive oil
750 g gourmet flat mushrooms,
roughly chopped
1 bunch spring onions, chopped
2 cloves garlic, chopped
1 tablespoon fresh rosemary
2 teaspoons lemon thyme
120 g Gladstone Encore Chévre
cheese, crumbled
120 g Kapiti Kokorangi
cheese, crumbled

Combine all ingredients for crust except cornmeal. Mix well. Roll dough on cornmeal to a circle approximately 30 cm in diameter. Place on an oven tray. To make the filling, heat oil and cook mushrooms, onions, garlic and herbs until all liquid evaporates, approximately 8 minutes. Cool and add cheeses. Spread mixture onto pastry, leaving 5 cm border. Pleat border up over filling. Bake at 200°C for 35 minutes until crust is deep golden. Serve hot or at room temperature. Serves 6.

TOADS LANDING, MASTERTON.

MILE-HIGH MARION PIE

CRUST
125 g gingernut biscuits, crushed

50 g butter

FILLING
300 g frozen marionberries

½ cup sugar

2 egg whites

250 ml cream, whipped

fresh berries for garnish

Prepare crust by mixing biscuits and butter together. Press onto base of spring-form tin and bake in oven for 10 minutes. To make filling, beat berries, sugar and egg whites together in bowl of an electric mixer for approximately 15 minutes until sugar has dissolved. Fold in the whipped cream. Pour over biscuit base and freeze. To serve, remove from tin and decorate the top with fresh berries. Serves 6.

TOADS LANDING, MASTERTON.

SCENIC AND AGRICULTURAL

This Wairarapa field south of Masterton soaks up the long summer season. Masterton is the centre of the prosperous Wairarapa, which combines rural beauty, industrial growth and a flourishing art scene. The community, which is approximately 100 km northeast of Wellington, can

be reached via an Upper Hutt to Featherston, Greytown and Carterton route. Masterton hosts the annual Golden Shears competition, has a large Arts Centre and its Queen Elizabeth Park offers boating on the lake, an aquarium and a deer park. Nearby Tararua Forest Park and Honeycomb Rock have walkways, and there is a Wildlife Centre at Mount Bruce.

HAWKE'S BAY FRUIT TERRINE

*a selection of fresh berries -
strawberries, raspberries,
blueberries, about 3 cups
1 cup sparking white wine
2 nips of Blue Curacao
2 nips of Peach Schnapps
(or other fruit liqueur)
100 ml water
200 g caster sugar
5 teaspoons powdered gelatine
3 oranges, peeled and segmented
200 g green grapes, halved*

**Prepare berries by removing
stalks. Place all liquid in a
heavy-bottomed pot, add sugar
and bring to the boil. Simmer
for 2-3 minutes. Dissolve
gelatine powder as per packet
instructions and add to liquid. Allow
to cool slightly. Build up layers of
fruit in the terrine and allow each
layer to set by placing in the freezer
before you put on the next layer.
When the terrine is full, leave to set in
refrigerator for 12-24 hours. To
remove from terrine, run the outside
under hot water and carefully turn out
onto a board or tray so it is easy to
cut. Serve two thin slices per person.
Serves about 6.**

VIDAL WINERY BRASSERIE,
HASTINGS.

SEA OF BLOSSOMS

Below, pink-blossomed fruit trees create the exhilaration of springtime in Hastings. Just 20 km southwest of Napier, Hastings lies on the Heretaunga Plains and is known for abundant fruit harvests, food processing and wine making. Areas near the Ngaruroro, Tutaekuri and Tukituki Rivers are especially fertile. Each year Hastings celebrates a Wine Festival, a Blossom Festival and a Highland Games. The region has several lovely parks as well as trout fishing, water rafting, jet boating and horse trekking. Nearby Cape Kidnappers has one of the world's three known mainland gannet colonies.

LEMON-HERBED LAMB ROULADE WITH CHARGRILLED AUBERGINE

4 lamb backstraps

CHERMOULA
2 cloves garlic
½ teaspoon each chilli, cracked pepper, sumac (lemon spice)
½ cup each coriander leaves, parsley
¼ cup mint
1½ teaspoons preserved lemon (lemon zest if not available)
¼ cup olive oil

AUBERGINE STUFFING
2 aubergines (eggplants)
1 onion, finely sliced
1 cup breadcrumbs
3 teaspoons chermoula seasoning

BALSAMIC SYRUP
3 tablespoons balsamic vinegar
100 g sugar

RED WINE REDUCTION
1 onion
6 cloves garlic
1 red capsicum
1 tablespoon olive oil
2 tomatoes, chopped
½ cup balsamic vinegar
2 tablespoons port
750 ml Cabernet Sauvignon wine

CHILLI GARNISH
4 jalapeño chillies
80 g feta cheese
12 rocket leaves

To prepare lamb, beat out the lamb with a meat hammer until flat. To prepare chermoula, finely chop all ingredients, season to taste and add olive oil. To prepare aubergine stuffing, slice aubergines and chargrill until golden and cooked. Once cooled, dice finely. Fry the onion until crisp and golden, toast breadcrumbs and mix all ingredients together, season to taste.

Lay a line of the stuffing along the lamb lengthwise and roll up to enclose the stuffing. Tie lamb with string. Marinate by covering in chermoula mix (best left overnight).

Red wine reduction: sweat onions, garlic and capsicum in olive oil on low heat. Add tomatoes, vinegar, port and wine and reduce by half. Strain through a sieve. Reduce to 1 cup.

To prepare chilli garnish, slice chilli down one side. Scoop out the seeds. Chargrill until skin is slightly blackened. Stuff each chilli with 20 g of feta cheese.

To serve, cook lamb on medium heat for 15-20 minutes. Heat red wine reduction and warm chillies in the oven at the last minute.

Slice each piece of lamb into three. Remove string and stand upright on plate. Cover with heated red wine sauce. Drizzle balsamic syrup around sauce and top lamb with 3 pieces of rocket and the grilled chilli.

Serves 4.

ANATOLES CAFÉ, NAPIER.

PANFRIED BLUE NOSE TOPPED WITH A SMOKED SALMON MOUSSE

---

300 g smoked salmon

6 tablespoons cream

20 sprigs of dill (keep 8 aside for garnish)

salt and pepper

800 g fresh Blue Nose

lemon pepper

50 g butter

½ cup fish stock

1 tablespoon dry white wine

50 g capers

1 lemon

1 tablespoon brown sugar

To make salmon mousse, purée salmon in a food processor. Add three-quarters of the cream and half of the dill (freshly chopped). Season to taste with salt and pepper. Mix to a smooth consistency. Place mixture into a piping bag and keep aside. To prepare fish, pre-heat oven to 200°C. Season the Blue Nose with lemon pepper and salt. Place butter in an ovenproof frying pan and heat until light brown. Quickly sear fish on both sides. Add half the fish stock and top fish with salmon mousse. Place frying pan in oven and bake for 7-10 minutes. Prepare sauce by placing the remainder of the fish stock, wine, capers, chopped dill, juice and zest of 1 lemon and brown sugar in a saucepan. Bring to the boil and season with salt and pepper. Add remainder of cream and reduce to a nice consistency. Spoon sauce onto 4 pre-heated plates. Place fish on top, garnish with fresh dill and salmon slices. Serve immediately. Serves 4.

BAYSWATER ON THE BEACH, NAPIER.

A DECORATIVE FLAIR

A coastal port, Napier was rebuilt in an art-deco style after it was demolished in the 1931 earthquake. The style is nurtured by the city's Art Deco Trust, and there is an Art Deco Walk and Art Deco Weekend, celebrating the city's architectural flavour. In Napier you can find house and wine tours, café crawls and jazz and vintage car festivals. A number of parks and plantings (see pages 84 & 85) add to the atmosphere, including the Norfolk

JOUE DE BOEUF (BEEF CHEEKS IN ALE)

1 kg trimmed beef cheeks

salt and pepper

1 medium carrot

1 medium onion

2 cloves garlic

small handful of fresh herbs (bay leaves, thyme, rosemary, sage)

2 tablespoons tomato paste

300 ml bottle ale or Guinness

300 ml water

Pine-lined Marine Parade, the Botanical Gardens and McLean, Tiffen and Trelernoe Parks. The Kennedy Park Rose Gardens supply a tropical ambience created by double rows of palms planted on each side of Kennedy Road. One of the oldest cities in the region, Napier is also the largest, with an atmosphere reminiscent of a British seaside resort. In the Napier suburb of Ahuriri is the Iron Pot Inlet, once used by early whalers but now an anchorage for small craft. Home of Marineland and the Hawke's Bay Aquarium, Napier also has energetic horticulture and winemaking industries as does Hastings.

Cut meat into large chunks and lightly season.

Pan-fry meat in a heavy pan until brown and sealed on all sides.

Remove meat and reserve. Rinse pan. Cut vegetables into bite-size pieces. Place meat back into the pan with vegetables, garlic and herbs and cover with tomato paste, ale (or red wine) and an equal amount of water. Cover and bake in the oven at 180°C for 2½ hours. You may need to add more liquid from time to time.

Remove lid and continue cooking for at least another hour (perhaps as much as two) until the meat is tender and will melt in your mouth. Once cooking is finished there should be enough left to serve your guests!

Serve with creamed potatoes, pasta, rice or polenta.

A crispy salad is also good.

Serves 4.

PIERRE SUR LE QUAI, NAPIER.

Previous pages: Clive Square in Napier.
Left: The Rothman's Building, Napier.
Described as a jewel of art deco, it was
built in 1933.

MANAWATU & WELLINGTON

THE WELLINGTON-MANAWATU REGION takes in the fast-paced capital city of New Zealand and its scenic harbour, pictured on these pages. It also includes the curving Kapiti Coast, the fertile inland valleys of the Manawatu and north as far as Wanganui, the first place we stopped. There we discovered a superb baked cream with the flavours and aromas of fresh pineapple and ginger. We drove south through fertile inland valleys where herds of dairy animals, sheep, lambs and stud sheep were fattening on lush pastures. In Palmerston North, known for Massey University's agricultural research, we indirectly benefited from their work when we dined on tender prime beef fillet garnished with pine-nut pesto and a flavoursome Cumberland sauce. A little way south in Te Horo, we sampled fresh crayfish dressed with a red capsicum mayonnaise, and then travelled to the Kapiti Coast. Nearby the coast the Horowhenua area is sculpted by rivers flowing down from the Tararuas such as the Ohau, the Otaki, the Manawatu and the Waikanae. We stopped awhile in the town of Waikanae to taste a sultry combination of chicken breast, avocado and strawberry sauce. We expected to find many good restaurants to choose from in Wellington, and we weren't disappointed. Included are recipes for a luscious scampi risotto and a sophisticated boudin blanc. You'll love every one!

CHICKEN FILLED WITH OLIVES, CHEESE & SUNDRIED TOMATOES

1 chicken breast
4 olives
50 g cheese
2 sundried tomatoes

Pre-heat oven to 160°C. Cut a pocket into the chicken breast, then fill with the olives, cheese and sundried tomatoes. Bake in oven for about 20 minutes, then place on confit of vegetables.
Serves 1.

CONFIT OF VEGETABLES
1 each red, yellow and green capsicum
2 onions, chopped
8 cloves garlic, chopped
¾ cup olive oil
salt and pepper

Cut the vegetables into strips, then place on oven tray with garlic, onion, oil, salt and pepper. Cover with foil and cook in oven at 160°C for about 20 minutes.

MICHAEL'S RESTAURANT, WANGANUI.

PINEAPPLE & GINGER BAKED CREAM

BAKED CREAM

2 cups cream

2 egg yolks

3 whole eggs

150 g sugar

100 g canned pineapple, chopped

60 g crystallised ginger, chopped

Mix all ingredients together, then place into small moulds and bake in a water bath in the oven for about 20-30 minutes at 170°C. Serves 4-6.

CITRUS SYRUP

2 oranges

2 limes

1 lemon

1 grapefruit

1 cup sugar

1.5 litres water

Cut all the fruit into quarters. Place into a saucepan with sugar and water, bring to the boil, then simmer for about 1-1½ hours or until the liquid reaches syrup thickness.

MICHAEL'S RESTAURANT, WANGANUI.

BEEF FILLET WITH PESTO & A BEETROOT CUMBERLAND SAUCE

PESTO

1 cup pine nuts

4 cups fresh basil leaves

1 teaspoon sea salt

¼ cup olive oil

3 cloves garlic

1 teaspoon freshly ground black pepper

1½ cups grated Parmesan cheese

BÉARNAISE SAUCE

2 shallots, chopped

6 peppercorns, crushed

1 tablespoon fresh tarragon

1 tablespoon balsamic vinegar

3 egg yolks

200 g butter

salt and pepper

sprig of chervil, chopped

BEETROOT CUMBERLAND SAUCE

2 shallots, chopped

½ cup redcurrant jelly

1 tablespoon lemon juice

2 tablespoons each port, balsamic vinegar

juice of 1 orange

1 large beetroot, grated

¼ cup red wine

1–1½ kg beef fillet

For pesto, pre-heat the oven to 180°C. Place pine nuts on a baking sheet and roast them until golden brown. Set aside until cool. Wash basil leaves, spin dry, then place in a food processor or blender. Add the salt and olive oil. Process for 30 seconds, then add garlic, pine nuts, pepper and Parmesan cheese. Process to a smooth paste, adding a little more oil if necessary. Make a fine but not runny pesto.

Store pesto covered with a little extra oil to prevent the basil from discolouring. The pesto will keep in the refrigerator for 1 week. Makes 2-3 cups. To make the Béarnaise Sauce, make a reduction with the shallots, peppercorns, tarragon and vinegar. Once reduced, pass through a sieve. Whisk the yolks and reduction in a bowl over boiling water until aerated. Gradually whisk in the melted butter and season to taste with salt, pepper and chopped chervil. To make the Beetroot Cumberland Sauce, sweat off shallots, add remainder of ingredients, bring to a simmer and reduce by a quarter. Leave to cool and pass through a sieve.

To prepare the beef, roast the fillet for 15-20 minutes at 190°C. Serve in slices with pesto, Béarnaise and Beetroot Cumberland Sauce. Serves 6.

CAFÉ VAVASSEUR,
PALMERSTON NORTH.

SMOKED SALMON
TIMBALE

250 g light sour cream
250 g light cream cheese
200 g smoked salmon
¼ teaspoon each dill, nutmeg, lemon juice
salt and pepper
1 teaspoon gelatine
Mesclun leaves
herbs
avocado
kumara chips

Mix sour cream and cream cheese
with half the smoked salmon in a
food processor, add seasonings and
gelatine dissolved in a little water.
Place in lined timbale moulds.
When set, place on serving plates
surrounded with mesclun leaves,
garnished with the herbs, other salad
ingredients and kumara chips. Dress
with a light orange vinaigrette.
Serves 6-8.

THE BATHHOUSE CAFÉ & BAR,
PALMERSTON NORTH.

On pages 92 & 93: *The Hay Garden in Palmerston North - just one of the lovely parklike settings in that city. You will also find the International Rose Trial Grounds at Esplanade Gardens; and the Pohangina Domain plus gardens and fountains in the Square. The Square is in the heart of Palmerston North and also includes the Manawatu Art Gallery, the Science Centre and the Manawatu Museum. Massey University is located in Palmerston North, famed for the agricultural research ongoing at AgResearch Grasslands, the Palmerston North Seed Testing Station, the NZ Dairy Research Institute, and the NZ Dairy Board's Awahuri Artificial Breeding Centre. The city has its lighter side as well, with three live theatres contributing to its cultural scene.*

SMOKED SALMON WITH RICOTTA CHEESE & GARLIC CROUTONS

VINAIGRETTE
2 tablespoons honey
½ cup olive oil
¼ cup white wine vinegar

CROUTONS
2 cloves garlic
50 g butter, melted
4 slices white bread
chopped parsley

SALMON
rocket leaves
endive
250 g ricotta cheese
8 large slices smoked salmon
fresh basil to garnish

To make the vinaigrette, combine all ingredients well. To make the croutons, crush garlic and add to butter. Remove crusts from bread and slice diagonally. Brush generously with garlic butter. Bake for 10 minutes at 180°C or until crisp. To assemble, arrange a bed of rocket and endive. Place a spoonful of ricotta in the centre. Arrange croutons, then salmon, then ricotta. Repeat again with remaining ingredients. Drizzle vinaigrette over salmon and croutons and garnish with freshly sliced basil. Serves 4.

CAFÉ VAVASSEUR, PALMERSTON NORTH.

Lush hydrangea and surrounding garden in Palmerston North are framed with exquisite stillness. Such gardens can be found throughout Palmerston North, offering rest for the eye and mind - a truly serene background for family occasions and meals.

POACHED CRAYFISH HALVES WITH ROASTED RED CAPSICUM MAYONNAISE

½ lemon
1 bay leaf
6 peppercorns
sprig of parsley
3 live crayfish
basil, roasted red capsicums, roasted red
capsicum mayonnaise, cherry tomatoes
and limes to garnish

Three-quarters fill a large preserving pan or stock pot with water and bring to the boil. Add lemon, bay leaf, peppercorns and parsley. In another large container or sink, drown the crayfish in cold water. (If they are dead before they go in the boiling water, the legs will stay intact.) Plunge the crayfish head first into the boiling water for 10 minutes. The water must cover the crayfish. Remove crayfish and chill. While crays are still cold, split through the tail and body and clean. To serve, arrange crayfish on a large platter on a bed of basil. Accompany with roasted red capsicum, roasted red capsicum mayonnaise (see facing page), cherry tomatoes and fresh limes. Serve with crusty bread and Chardonnay (Ata Rangi 1994 Craighall Chardonnay is recommended).
Serves 6.

ROASTED RED CAPSICUM MAYONNAISE

1 red capsicum
1 clove garlic, peeled
2 egg yolks
salt and pepper
juice of 1 lime
a dash of Tabasco Sauce
1 cup olive oil

Cut red capsicum in half and de-seed. Grill skin side up until skin looks charred and bubbly. Cool, peel and chop. Place red capsicum, garlic, egg yolks, salt, pepper, lime juice, Tabasco and ¼ cup olive oil into food processor bowl with metal blade fitted. Blend until smooth. Pour remaining olive oil very slowly through the feed tube with the food processor running.
Taste for seasoning.

RUTH PRETTY CATERING & COOKING SCHOOL, TE HORO

CHICKEN BREAST WITH STRAWBERRY SAUCE

CHICKEN

4 skinned and boned
chicken breasts
flour
1 egg, lightly beaten
breadcrumbs
oil or butter
avocado to garnish
sprig of fresh mint & fresh
strawberries to garnish

STRAWBERRY SAUCE

¼ cup sugar
2 cups water
200 g strawberries
1 tablespoon cornflour

GARNISH

mint leaves
fresh strawberries

Crumb chicken in flour, egg and breadcrumbs. Pan-fry in oil or butter to sear then bake in oven for 15 minutes. Slice and arrange on a sliced avocado. To make sauce, boil sugar in the water, add the strawberries and thicken with cornflour mixed to a paste with a little water. Pour over chicken and garnish with mint and fresh strawberries.
Serves 4.

COUNTRY LIFE RESTAURANT,
WAIKANAE.

WONDERFUL WAIKANAE

From picturesque and historic Pukerua Bay, Highway 1 follows the sometimes rocky and spectacular Kapiti Coast to the thriving community of Waikanae. It is favoured by many retired people, some of whom were enticed by hopes of angling for trout in the Waikanae River, said to be

good sport and good eating. The township looks out at Kapiti Island, Waikanae Beach is sandy and lupin covered, and there is also a pine plantation nearby. The area includes a number of enjoyable recreational activities such as walks in the Nga Manu Bird Sanctuary, the Mangaone Walkway or other bush reserves and wetland areas. Visiting the local pottery studio is another pleasant way to spend your time.

Pukerua Bay on the Kapiti Coast, South of Waikanae.

SCAMPI CON RISOTTO ALLO ZAFFERANO E FRITTATA DI SPINACI

(SCAMPI WITH SAFFRON RISOTTO & SPINACH FRITTATA)

12 large simu scampi
salt and pepper
4 tablespoons olive oil
2 teaspoons chopped parsley
4 leaves basil plus 4 double leaves
1 fresh tomato, diced
2 eggs
1/2 cup cream
100 g cooked spinach
200 g rice (Arborio short grain)
3/4 cup fish stock
pinch saffron
4 tablespoons Parmesan cheese
knob butter
1 teaspoon soy sauce

Cut scampi from the back, clean head, season with salt, pepper and oil, and place in a baking dish. Combine parsley, basil, tomato, teaspoon olive oil, salt and pepper and fill scampi heads with mixture. Beat eggs with cream, add chopped spinach, season with salt and pepper. With a medium round pastry cutter form four frittata. Bake approximately 3-5 minutes. Keep warm. Cook rice with fish stock and saffron until soft, about 15 minutes. Add Parmesan cheese and butter. Bake scampi in pre-heated oven at 180°C for about 5 minutes. Place rice on middle of four pre-heated plates, garnish with spinach frittata and arrange three scampi on top. Mix soy sauce with 1 teaspoon olive oil and pour over. Garnish with double basil leaves and serve.

IL CASINO RISTORANTE,
WELLINGTON.

CRAB-STUFFED MUSHROOM WITH ROASTED CAPSICUM & BASIL VINAIGRETTE

FILLING

¼ cup each melted butter, Parmesan
cheese, grated cheddar cheese
2 tablespoons sliced spring onions
1 tablespoon chopped parsley
¼ teaspoon cayenne pepper
freshly ground black pepper
¼ cup breadcrumbs
500 g crab meat, picked over for bits
of shell
8 mushroom caps, stems carefully cut off

VINAIGRETTE

½ cup roasted red capsicum
¼ cup fresh basil leaves
2 cloves garlic
salt and freshly-ground black pepper
1 tablespoon each lemon juice,
balsamic vinegar
1 cup olive oil

Melt the butter in the microwave. Add
the remaining ingredients, combining
well. Fold in crab meat carefully and
set aside. Mould a portion of the crab
meat mixture onto each mushroom cap.
Bake at 180°C for approximately 12
minutes. To make vinaigrette, blend all
ingredients except oil in a food
processor. Drizzle the oil in a slow
steady stream until the sauce is
combined. To assemble, place two
stuffed mushrooms on top of a crouton
and drizzle with the vinaigrette.
Garnish with a basil leaf.
Makes 4 large entrée or 4 light lunches.

LOGAN BROWN, WELLINGTON.

BOUDIN BLANC: CHICKEN, SWEETBREADS & MUSHROOMS

250 g calves' sweetbreads
30 g dried cépe mushrooms
4 tablespoons finely chopped parsley
100 g finely chopped onion
1 tablespoon butter
500 g chicken breast meat, diced
2 teaspoons salt
1 whole egg
2 egg whites
¼ teaspoon each, ground nutmeg, white pepper
500 ml cream
2 metres sausage skins

THE DAY BEFORE

Soak sweetbreads in cold water with 1 tablespoon of salt for 1 hour. Simmer in a court bouillon (stock) for 5-8 minutes, until firm. Drain. While still warm, peel and cut into small pieces. Place in refrigerator.

ON THE DAY

Soak mushrooms in hot water for 1 hour. Drain, dry and finely chop. Mix with the parsley and set aside.

SEASIDE BEAUTY

Above are stylish homes and high-rise apartment buildings on a steep hillside in the Wellington suburb of Oriental Bay. Known for its sunny location and magnificent views over Wellington Harbour, the locale is a popular place for boating and swimming. Its beach is not the natural

Sauté the diced onion in 1 tablespoon of butter until golden. Set aside. Make a purée of the chicken flesh in a food processor, adding the salt, egg, egg white, seasonings and onion as the chicken reduces to a purée. Add the cream last, emulsifying only a little more. Too much speed will cause the cream to curdle. Transfer to a bowl and add the mushrooms, parsley and sweetbreads. Stuff the sausage skins with the mixture. Be careful not to overfill the skins or to leave any air holes. Once the skins are full, twist the sausages into lengths. An easy way is to tie each end with string. Gently poach the sausages at 85°C in a pot of salted water. Do not boil. Allow the sausages to cool then place in refrigerator. Do not keep for more than three days. Serve grilled with pommes purée, creamed spinach and chicken jus.
Serves 8-10.

BOULCOTT STREET BISTRO, WELLINGTON.

Left: A dazzling day of sunshine at Oriental Bay. Its homes and luxury high-rise apartments enjoy stunning bay views as well as proximity to the city centre.

result of tidal action, but has a different history, being composed of ballast conveyed to the Wellington area on sailing vessels. Oriental Parade itself is named for one of the New Zealand Company's sailing ships and is part of Wellington's scenic Marine Drive. This route begins from the Parade, includes Miramar Peninsula, Island Bay, Owhiro Bay and also passes Wellington Airport.

MARLBOROUGH & NELSON

NELSON AND MARLBOROUGH occupy the top of the South Island, which is carved by the beautiful Tasman and Golden Bays. We began our trip in the Picton, Blenheim and Cloudy Bay area, eating at excellent restaurants and enjoying local brews and award-winning wines with our meals. (The photo on this page shows the Brancott Valley vines just south of Woodbourne in the Blenheim region.) We ate scallops in Blenheim that were accented with lime and served on crispy noodles, and in Havelock we just had to taste a thick and creamy mussel chowder. Near Havelock, sea ferries meander through the inlets and sounds of northeast Marlborough, and farther north are the Abel Tasman and Nelson Lakes National Parks, the Heaphy Track and the upwelling Waikoropupu Springs. In the Nelson region we feasted our eyes on the artistry of Nelson potters, who turn local clays into prized ceramics, and we satisfied our chocolate lust with a sensationally-gooey chocolate mud tart. Motueka is one of New Zealand's main fruit-growing areas, and other delicacies such as local free range eggs, smoked salmon and cheeses, as well as trout and seafood are cooked into tempting fare. Every recipe here is more than delicious!

The Marlborough Sounds, wondrous isles and cliffs created by glacial ice gouging deep passages in the land which were later filled by the rising ocean. Blenheim lies south of D'Urville Island, which is part of the ragged eastern border of the Tasman Bay and the western edge of Marlborough Sounds.

CHANNEL CHAMPION

D'Urville Island was named for and by Jules Sebastien Cesar Dumont d'Urville, who explored Tasman Bay during a three-year exploration of New Zealand. One fascinating Maori legend attached to the island refers to Hinepoupou, whose philandering husband abandoned her on Kapiti Island off the coast of the North Island near Wellington. After summoning the assistance of the atua, she survived the mighty Cook Strait and reached the safety of the Brothers on the eastern reaches of Marlborough Sounds. According to the legend, Hinepoupou then made her way from that lonely place of seabirds and tuatara lizards back to her home on D'Urville Island.

ROASTED GLOBE ARTICHOKE WITH SUNDRIED TOMATO PESTO & FRESH PARMESAN

ARTICHOKES

3 globe artichokes

50 g sundried tomato pesto

olive oil

Parmesan cheese, dry and fresh

3 cherry tomatoes

3 cloves garlic

SUNDRIED TOMATO PESTO

1 bunch basil

3 tablespoons toasted pine nuts

2 cloves garlic

2 tablespoons finely grated Parmesan

2 tablespoons sundried tomatoes

3 tablespoons olive oil

To prepare the artichokes, blanch until soft throughout, peel off leaves, cut artichokes in halves, place into a roasting dish and drizzle olive oil over each half.

Season and sprinkle each half with Parmesan cheese, half a cherry tomato and half a clove of garlic. Roast for 15 minutes at 150°C.

To make the tomato pesto, combine all ingredients except the oil in a food processor and work until chopped. With the motor running, add oil in a steady stream to give a smooth pesto.

Garnish with freshly shaved Parmesan.

Serves 3.

HOTEL D'URVILLE, BLENHEIM.

MARLBOROUGH MUSSEL PASTA IN LEMON & RED WINE SAUCE

1 onion, thinly sliced
1 clove garlic, minced
3 tablespoons oil
850 g can tomatoes,
drained, juice reserved
¼ cup tomato purée
1 lemon, thinly sliced,
pips removed
1 teaspoon dried oregano
1 tablespoon coarsely
chopped fresh basil
½ teaspoon coarsely
ground pepper
¼ teaspoon red
pepper flakes
2 dozen Greenlip mussels,
steamed and removed from shells
1 cup dry red wine
450 g tagliatelle or fettuccine

Sauté onion and garlic in oil. Add all
ingredients except mussels,
wine and pasta.
Simmer for 25 minutes.
Add wine, simmer until sauce
thickens. Add mussels, whole or
quartered depending on personal
preference and simmer. Cook pasta in
a large saucepan of boiling water.
Toss sauce with pasta. If sauce
becomes too dry while simmering,
reserved cooking liquid from steamed
mussels or juice from tomatoes may
be added as required.
Serves 4.

AN EPICUREAN AFFAIR,
BLENHEIM.

EMINENT ESTATES AND BOUTIQUE LABELS

Blenheim can be reached by travelling 29 km south of Picton on Highway 1 or 117 km from Nelson along Highway 6. Both wend their way through the Richmond Range and cross the Wairau River to reach the sunny Wairau Plains, which face Cloudy Bay. Here, leafy vineyards planted in the well-drained local soils have flourished, and Blenheim vintages are becoming known worldwide. Recently six stamps were printed to honour the success of New Zealand wines, and on the face of one of those is Cloudy Bay Wineries.

Grapevines at Blenheim. More than 20 prospering wineries have been established in the Blenheim region.

NELSON SCALLOPS WITH A GINGER & LIME CONCASSÉ ON CRISPY NOODLES

SCALLOPS

1 tablespoon olive oil
8-10 large Nelson scallops
1 teaspoon liquid honey
¼ cup white wine
salt and pepper
freshly chopped coriander
juice of ½ lemon

CONCASSÉ

1 small red onion
1 large red tomato
5 mm slice of ginger root
juice and zest of 1 lime
2 tablespoons balsamic vinegar
1 tablespoon olive oil

NOODLES *dry egg noodles*

GARNISH *chives*

To prepare scallops, heat a medium-size heavy frypan. Add olive oil. Once oil begins to spit, add scallops. Gently sear each side, add honey, white wine, seasoning, coriander and lemon juice. Reduce liquid by half. To make the concassé, finely dice the red onion, remove flesh from tomato by cutting into quarters and scooping flesh out. Dice the skin, grate ginger, add zest and lime juice. Bind with balsamic vinegar and oil. Soak the noodles for 10 minutes in warm water until soft, drain and pat dry. Deep-fry for 2 minutes. Arrange noodles in the middle of a plate and place scallops on noodles, spoon on concassé. Garnish with chives.

Serves 1-2.

HOTEL D'URVILLE, BLENHEIM.

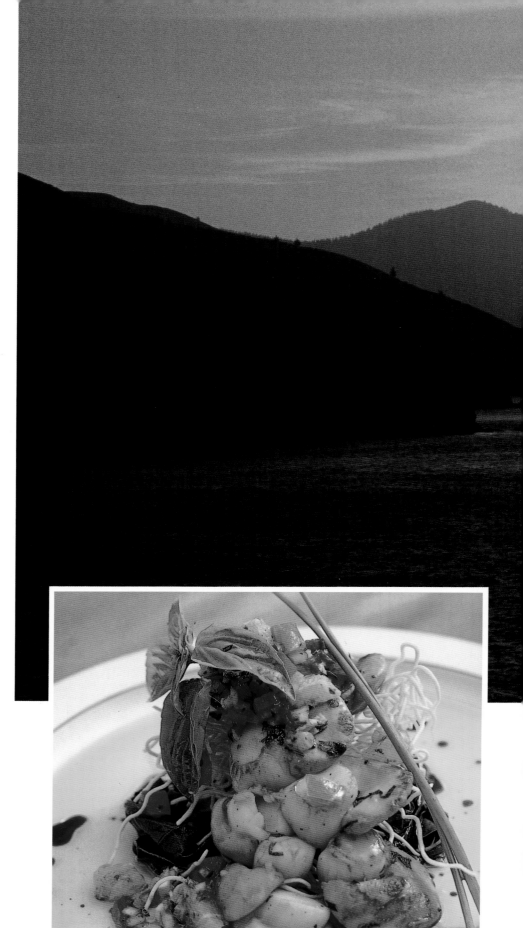

IN THE ARMS OF THE SEA

Highway 6 ripples its way from Nelson to Blenheim, crossing the Pelorus River, the Bryant Range and the wide, straight Wairau River. Roughly two-thirds of the way from Blenheim to Nelson are Havelock and Moenui, nestling in a bay of the Mahau Sound, at the head of the Pelorus Sound. Havelock is a centre for both freshwater and ocean anglers, and scallops are still plentiful. The town came into being after gold was discovered at Wakamarina in 1864, and, when the gold was exhausted, logging sustained the community. Now launches leave from Havelock on both business and pleasure trips. Visitors can enjoy guided sea kayaking trips and walks on the Nydia Track.

Before it vanishes, the sunset light lingers and plays on the waters and cliff faces of the Marlborough Sounds. Greenlip mussels, grown commercially in the Marlborough Sounds, are processed in Havelock. Shucked mussels are marinated or frozen for sale. Premium-grade bivalves are left in the half shell to be quick frozen for export or sale to restaurants.

MUSSEL CHOWDER

1 medium onion, diced
100 g butter
1 nip Galliano
1 teaspoon curry powder
2 teaspoons lemon juice
1 large carrot, diced
1 cup white sauce
seafood stock to taste
350 g mussel meat
extra milk if needed
salt and pepper to taste

WHITE SAUCE
50 g butter
¼ cup flour
1 cup milk

GARNISH
chopped parsley
whipped cream

Sauté onion in butter, add Galliano, curry powder and lemon juice. Steam cook carrots and add to onions. Make up white sauce and add to pot with seafood stock. Dice mussels and add last, adding extra milk if need be. Simmer for 15 minutes and serve, topped with whipped cream and chopped parsley. Serves 4.

THE DARLING DILL CAFÉ,
HAVELOCK.

SALMON CHAR SUI WRAPPED IN SEAWEED & OVEN BAKED

8 standard-sized sheets of nori (baked
seaweed)
1 punnet of snowpea sprouts
4 spring onions, cut in half lengthways
1 small carrot, peeled and julienned
4 sundried tomatoes or 2 normal
tomatoes, de-seeded and cut in strips.
300-400 g boneless, skinless salmon
fillet, cut in strips
1 jar of Lee Kum Kee Char Sui
Marinade (available from most
supermarkets)

DIPPING SAUCE
100 ml standard Kikkoman Soy Sauce
2 cloves garlic, chopped
1 teaspoon minced fresh ginger
juice of 1 lime
1 tablespoon sweet Thai chilli sauce

ARTISTS' SHOWCASE

The electric flash of sizzling lightning yellow from a gleaming platter. The exciting roughness of a raku-fired stoneware teapot. The gleam and shine of a twist of golden metal or the silvery matte of a burnished bracelet. The rich warmth of handwoven shawls and tasselled wall hangings. Surely Nelson is one of the most exciting places in New Zealand for those who love the creative arts. Do you like pots, paintings

Place the nori on a tea towel or a nori mat. Along the bottom one-third place the garnishes, ie snowpea sprouts, spring onions, carrots, salmon and tomatoes.

Drizzle a teaspoon of char sui sauce over top. Using the mat or tea towel roll up to form a large cigar shape or nori roll, seal the leading edge with a little water. Do the same with the other seven nori.

To make the dipping sauce, mix all ingredients together. Divide into 4 little ramekins or other suitable containers.

Heat oven to 180°C. Place the salmon nori rolls on a lightly greased baking tray and bake for 3-4 minutes only.

Slice in half lengthways and arrange attractively on four starter plates. Serve with dipping sauce and other accompaniments of your choice. Serves 4 as a starter.

BOAT SHED CAFÉ, NELSON.

or pendants? Wood carving or china painting? Weaving, wire sculpture or wool toys? All these and more can be found in the flourishing studios and galleries inside and outside Nelson. And the creative zest doesn't stop here - there are creative adventure tours and innovative breweries, temptingly prepared food at fine establishments plus novel wines and new methods of food processing. The Nelson lifestyle is a happy blend of sunny skies and scenic beauty and, as throughout New Zealand, the friendliness of people who enjoy their way of life.

RAVIOLI OF SCALLOPS WITH CAPER BEURRE BLANC SAUCE

CAPER SAUCE

2 tablespoons capers

2 tablespoons white wine vinegar

½ bay leaf

juice of ½ lemon

150 g unsalted butter

salt and black pepper (to taste)

RAVIOLI

50 g butter

1 cup finely chopped onion

4 cloves garlic, finely chopped

½ large red and yellow capsicum, chopped

1 tablespoon each chopped basil, chopped dill

¼ cup chopped parsley

juice and grated zest of 1 lemon

salt and freshly ground black pepper

32 wonton wrappers

16-32 scallops (depending on size)

To make the sauce, gently squeeze the juice from the capers into a saucepan. Reserve capers. Add all the remaining ingredients, except the butter and seasoning. Bring to a rapid boil and reduce until only one tablespoon remains. Remove the pan from the heat and whisk in the butter to form an emulsified sauce.

Add the capers and season to taste
with black pepper. Keep warm.
To make the ravioli, melt the butter in
a fairly large skillet. Add the onion,
garlic and capsicum and sweat until
soft, approximately 3 minutes.
Remove from heat and add all the
herbs, lemon juice and zest. Season
to taste with salt and pepper.
Arrange 16 wonton wrappers on a
clean, dry bench and place
$1/2$ teaspoon of mixture in the
centre of each. Place a scallop or
two (depending on size) on the
mixture, keep the edges clean.
Gently moisten around the edge of
each wrapper with water. This will
allow the top wonton wrapper to
become glued to the bottom one.
Take care not to use too much water
or the wrapper can become soggy.
Meanwhile bring a large pot of salted
water to a rolling boil. Drop one
ravioli at a time into the water, try
not to let the water come off the boil.
Eight at a time will be enough. A little
oil in the water should prevent the
ravioli from sticking together.
Gently simmer for approximately
3 minutes and carefully remove with
a slotted spoon and arrange
decoratively in the centre of four
warmed plates or pasta bowls. Spoon
a little sauce on each ravioli.
Garnish as desired.
Serves 4.

Boat Shed Café, Nelson.

PEACE AND QUIET

Pelorus Bridge is 45 minutes east of Nelson and is close to Canvastown, where the closet gold miner can induge a secret whim to pan for gold. There are many walking tracks in the area, pleasant tearooms, untouched native forest and proximity to the Pelorus Sound and launch trips into the Sound. Those seeking the refreshing solitude of casting a lure for wary trout will enjoy themselves here as well as those seeking new sights. Stunning views are all along the scenic Queen Charlotte drive, and from the reserve area walking trails lead to the Maungatapu and Matai Valleys.

The Pelorus Bridge Scenic Reserve has a tranquil atmosphere for outdoor enthusiasts.

GREEN ENCLAVES PRESERVED...

Established as the New Zealand Company's second settlement in 1841, Nelson is now well known for its pleasant climate and attractive lifestyle. One component of this lifestyle is the number of parks and gardens in or nearby Nelson. There is Isel Park with its well established trees, rhododendrons and azaleas and the Botanical Reserves with a tangle of paths up to Botanical Hill and the view of Tasman Bay. There are the Queen's Gardens, Mount Richmond Forest Park, Anzac Park and Rutherford Park, which honours the nuclear physicist Lord Rutherford of

CHOCOLATE MUD TART

2 sheets pre-rolled butter pastry or your favourite pastry base
100 g unsalted butter, chopped
275 g block dark chocolate, chopped
½ cup double cream
½ cup brown sugar
3 eggs
¾ cup ground almonds
fresh summer berries for decoration

Roll out pastry sheets to line the base and sides of a 24 cm diameter loose bottomed flan tin. Refrigerate while preparing the filling. Place butter, chocolate, cream and half the brown sugar in the top part of a double boiler. Allow to melt over simmering water. Stir until cool. Beat the eggs and remaining brown sugar together for 2 minutes until light and frothy. Mix into cooled chocolate mixture, fold through the ground almonds. Pour filling into prepared flan tin and cook at 180°C for 30-40 minutes. Serves 10-12.

KORURANGI CAFÉ, NELSON.

Nelson. In Richmond Forest Park those of active persuasion can stride along the old gold-miners' track, the Waikakaho-Cullen Creek Track or visit Lake Chalice or Mount Richmond. There are walks near Dun Mountain, the Hacket River and Cable Bay, and lovely drives lead to Nelson Haven and the Davis lookout on the Post Hills. The city is also in close proximity to the new Kahurangi National Park and to the Abel Tasman and Nelson Lakes National Parks. In Kahurangi, the second largest National Park in New Zealand, visitors can see Nettlebed and Bulmer, the country's deepest and longest caves. And the renowned Heaphy, Wangapeka and Leslie/Karamea Tracks run through Kahurangi Park.

Central Nelson provides many tree-shaded settings for a pleasant walk or an evening's reverie on a bench by the river.

Following pages show a crescent of beach in Abel Tasman National Park and a Motueka scene with statue.

GOLDEN BAY SCALLOPS SERVED WITH PORT NICHOLSON BEURRE BLANC SAUCE

SHELLS
400 g flaky puff pastry
2 leeks
24 scallops

SAUCE
approx 75 g Port Nicholson cheese
½ cup cream
½ cup good fish stock
1 teaspoon lemon juice
seasoning to taste

**Roll pastry out 5 mm thick.
Prepare four scallop shells from flaky
puff pastry moulded inside
real scallop shells.
Blind bake at 200°C until cooked.
Cut leeks into julienne strips, season
and steam until tender. Steam
scallops for 2 minutes.
To prepare Port Nicholson Beurre
Blanc Sauce, place sauce
ingredients in pan.
Cook on moderate heat until sauce
thickens. Serve immediately over hot
scallops and leeks in pastry shells.
Serves 4 as a starter.**

GOTHIC GOURMET LICENSED
RESTAURANT & TAVERN,
MOTUEKA.

TAME EELS AND RIVERSIDE MEALS

The Tasman coastline is a visual feast of stern headlands and petite beaches of golden sand. Motueka was established on the west side of Tasman Bay just south of the Abel Tasman National Park. Fed by the Arthur and Hope ranges, the Motueka River flows through the town and empties into Tasman Bay. Motueka is full of tourist-oriented activities, including fishing, caving, flights to Abel Tasman, horse trekking, paragliding and skydiving, horticultural and winery tours, sailing, golfing and dining at riverside cafés. Visitors also enjoy the Abel Tasman Coastal Classic fun run, the Salt Water Baths, the January Riwaka Beerfest and the Abel Tasman Seal Swim. On the outskirts of Motueka, hops, tobacco, raspberries and other crops are cultivated, and several tobacco and hop research stations are located nearby. You can handfeed the tame eels and trout on the Anatoki River, or refresh yourself at such places as Ruby Bay Wines, the Redwood Cellars, the Neudorf Vineyards or at one of the many lodges, holiday and leisure parks, hotels and restaurants.

WEST COAST

DAMP BUT DELIGHTFUL, MAJESTIC AND MYSTERIOUS - the West Coast nestles against the western side of the Southern Alps. The Franz Josef Glacier, pictured here, is one of the mighty snowfed rivers of ice moving down from the main divide and the peaks of Mount Cook National Park. Fox Glacier is only 25 kilometres away. We began our tour in Murchison (inland and north of Westport), breakfasted on feather-light pancakes and dined on tender sweet and sour pork fillet in filo baskets. All the way south, we found breathtaking alpine passes, wild rivers, rainforests and estuaries and towns with friendly individualists who love their remote land. The West Coast's Heritage Highways made it simple to discover the great food on offer in Westland such as the Westport seafood medley and the bacon-flavoured loin of boar garnished with salmon cream. There is comfortable accommodation plus lots of local goodies like homemade breads, jams and yoghurt - even farm-fresh goat's milk! Seafood is grand, with salmon and trout plentiful. Venison, duck and whitebait can be sampled as well as New Zealand wines. Do travel here soon to meet the children and grandchildren of goldminers, loggers, coal miners and pioneers and to taste their flavoursome recipes!

SWEET & SOUR PORK BASKETS

SAUCE
1 onion, finely sliced
1 tablespoon oil
1 carrot
½ red capsicum
3 tablespoons cornflour
2 tablespoons soy sauce
¼ cup brown sugar
¼ cup wine vinegar
¾ cup water
2 tablespoons sherry
1 teaspoon chicken stock powder
½ cup pineapple juice
1 cup pineapple pieces

BASKETS
8 sheets filo
butter

PORK
24 slices from a fillet of pork

Sauté onion in oil until clear. Peel and slice carrot and capsicum into matchsticks. Add to onion and stir-fry for 5 minutes. Combine cornflour, soy sauce, sugar, vinegar, water, sherry, chicken stock powder and pineapple juice in a large microwave-proof bowl. Microwave uncovered on high power for 4 minutes, stirring twice. Add onion, carrot and capsicum. Stir well. Add pineapple pieces. Cook on high power for 90 seconds. To make the baskets, take two sheets of filo pastry. Brush one sheet with melted butter and lay on top of other sheet. Fold all four corners to the middle. Place folded edges down into a greased ramekin.

Repeat with remaining filo. Bake 10 minutes at 180°C. Remove filo basket from ramekin.

To prepare pork, cut 6 slices per basket from a fillet of pork. Fry both sides in 1 tablespoon oil on a high heat until pink juices show.

Put 1 tablespoon of sauce in the bottom of the basket, add the pork pieces and cover with hot sauce. Serves 4.

BEECHWOODS, MURCHISON.

PANCAKES BEECHWOODS STYLE

2 tablespoons sugar

1 egg

1 cup milk

1 teaspoon vanilla essence

pinch salt

1 1/2 cups flour

2 teaspoons cream of tartar

1 teaspoon baking soda

1 tablespoon butter

2 tablespoons boiling water

Beat egg with sugar until frothy. Add milk, vanilla essence and salt. Mix in flour, cream of tartar and baking soda, then add butter melted in the boiling water. Pour 1 cup of mix into a well-greased hot frypan. Turn when bubbles appear on the surface. Serve with slices of fresh fruit, dust with icing sugar and top with whipped cream. Makes 6-8.

BEECHWOODS, MURCHISON.

SEAFOOD MEDLEY

SAUCE

2 shallots or 1/2 onion,
finely diced
3/4 cup dry white wine
1/2 cup cream
150 g unsalted butter, cubed
1 teaspoon lemon juice
salt and pepper

MEDLEY

2 or 3 tiger prawns
150 g white fish fillets,
skinned and boned
3 whole mussels
1/2 crayfish tail
1/2 cup white wine
1/2 onion, diced
4 to 6 scallops

To make the sauce, simmer onion in a saucepan with wine until liquid has almost evaporated. Add cream and reduce until cream has thickened. Remove from heat, whisk in butter until a creamy sauce is produced. Add lemon juice and seasonings. Peel and de-vein prawns. Cut fish into 3 or 4 bite-size pieces. Remove any debris from mussels and wash. Cut crayfish tail into segments leaving shell on. Steam mussels in white wine and onion until they open. Keep warm. Grill all other fish until just cooked. Arrange on serving plate and pour sauce over, garnish and serve. Serves 2.

DIEGO'S RESTAURANT & BAR, WESTPORT.

Cape Foulwind, near Westport.

TAURANGA BAY CHILLI MUSSELS

2 *large brown onions*
1 *large carrot*
1 *stalk celery, diced*
1 *each, medium red, green capsicum*
4 *tablespoons olive oil*
6 *cloves garlic, crushed*
1 *cup canned whole peeled plum tomatoes*
4 *sprigs fresh basil*
1 *tablespoon fresh thyme*
1 *tablespoon fresh oregano*
3 *bay leaves*
fresh red chilli, finely chopped, to taste
sea salt flakes and freshly ground
black pepper to taste
12 *small Greenlip mussels*
or mussels in the 1/2 shell

Finely dice onion, carrot, celery and peppers. Heat olive oil in heavy-based stock pot then add onion, carrot, celery, capsicums and garlic. Fry gently until ingredients are softened. Do not let them brown. Add tomatoes, herbs and chilli. Add chilli in small amounts until you find the balance that is right for you. Bring to the boil and simmer very slowly for one hour with the lid off. Crush tomatoes with a masher to form a thickish sauce. Add salt and pepper to taste. Pour off amount you need into heavy-based fry pan. Place cleaned mussels into simmering sauce and serve when mussels open. (Discard any that remain closed). Do not overcook, or they will be tough. Serve immediately in large wide bowl with slices of French baguette to mop up all the sauce. Serves 2.

THE BAY HOUSE CAFÉ, TAURANGA BAY, WESTPORT.

LOIN OF WILD BOAR WRAPPED IN BACON WITH A VENISON SALAMI & SMOKED SALMON CREAM

400 g wild boar or pork loin
4 slices raw back bacon
50 g venison salami
salt and pepper
½ small onion, finely chopped
olive oil
100 ml white wine
50 g smoked salmon, diced
200 ml cream
25 g butter

Cut boar into 4 x 100 g pieces. Remove rind and fat from back bacon. Cut salami into matchstick-sized strips. Season the boar with salt and pepper in a hot pan for a few seconds each side. Wrap the boar in the bacon, holding in place with toothpicks. Place in a hot oven for 10-12 minutes. In the same pan cook the onions without browning in a drop of olive oil. Add the wine and reduce by half. Add the salami, salmon and cream and continue to reduce by a third. Shake in the butter while heating gently but do not allow to boil as the sauce will split. Adjust the seasoning to suit. Place the boar parcels on a warm plate, remove the toothpicks and pour the sauce over.
Serves 4.

TRAPPERS RESTAURANT, HOKITIKA.

Punakaiki, or Pancake Rocks, can be found at Dolomite Point, about an hour and a half drive from Hokitika.

Mount Cook, New Zealand's highest peak, towers 3753 metres above sea level. From its summit, a climber can look down on the Tasman, Fox and Franz Joseph Glaciers, the lush green bush of the national park, Lakes Pukaki and Tekapo, the Okarito Lagoon as well as lesser peaks such as Mounts Sefton, Tasman and Malte Brun. From the Mount Cook area, it is about 100 kilometres north to Hokitika. Near the town is an assortment of more than fifteen walkways and tracks, including the Hokitika Heritage Trail. Adventure touring, rural stays and nearly twenty arts and crafts shops also lure many tourists to the area. Hokitika has whitebaiting in season, a gold room, a glassblowing studio and greenstone-working studios as well as scenic drives offering spectacular views of the Southern Alps.

RICH HONEYED FRUIT CAKE

4 cups mixed dried fruit
1 cup whole almonds
½ cup honey
1¼ cups plain flour

Grease deep, 23-cm, round cake tin
and line base and sides with baking
paper. Combine all ingredients in
large bowl, stir until well combined.
Spread mixture into prepared tin.
Bake in slow oven at 150°C for about
1¼ hours. Cover hot cake tightly
with foil. Cool in pan. When cake is
cold, drizzle with melted chocolate.
Serve thinly sliced.

LAKE PARINGA CAFÉ,
LAKE PARINGA,
SOUTH WESTLAND.

*Below: The Lake Paringa Café is
now open and welcomes you to try
its delicious specialties.*

WEST COAST WHITEBAIT OMELET

(A well-seasoned omelet pan is essential for this recipe.)

1 teaspoon butter
¼ onion, finely diced
140 grams whitebait
1 small clove garlic, crushed
3 eggs
salt and pepper
freshly chopped herbs

Melt butter, add onion and sauté until soft and transparent (do not brown). Add whitebait and garlic, toss over gentle heat until cooked, add beaten eggs, salt, pepper and herbs. Cook quickly, moving continuously with a fork until lightly set. Remove from heat. Fold omelet out of pan. Sprinkle with freshly chopped herbs and lemon pepper.
Serves 1.

LAKE PARINGA CAFÉ,
LAKE PARINGA.

Left: Driftwood lies scattered in pleasing designs on a wide sandy beach near Haast. In southern Westland, Ship Creek and its walkways near Haast ramble through native Kahikatea forests and beside rugged coastlines.

Top left: Whitebaiters try their luck at a West Coast riverside.

KAIKOURA & CANTERBURY

THE PHOTO ON THESE TWO PAGES LOOKS WEST over the great Canterbury Plains of the South Island. Wide and fertile they stretch from the Southern Alps to the sea. In this part of our tour, we started in Kaikoura, no longer a whaling town but well known for the gentler sport of whale watching. You can also swim with seals or watch dusky dolphins frolic in the shelter of the Kaikoura Range. Eating is a marvellous experience, with recipes like seared crayfish tail heaped with mango and citrus salsa. The Fyffe Gallery is but one of a number of unique resorts: it has an art gallery, a country garden, a large courtyard and a handmade earthblock home with recycled timber and fittings. Next we travelled south to Christchurch, which offers many attractions like terraced houses, Cathedral Square, the casino, Hagley Park, the museum and the Botanical Gardens (recently converted to organic pest control). When we dined in Christchurch, the smoked salmon tartare parcels in sour cream and brandy were too good to resist! Historic Lyttelton was next, with reminders that the first Europeans to arrive in the South Island settled nearby. A harbour town with villas overlooking stunning views, its restaurant menus offered many temptations. Lastly we arrived in Timaru, where we found an appetising turkey salad with a robust honey, orange, mustard and vinegar dressing. We found many outdoor adventures and indoor dining pleasures in Canterbury.

SEARED CRAYFISH TAIL WITH MANGO CITRUS SALSA

SALSA

2 mangoes or 1 x 440 g can
¹/₂ red onion
¹/₂ each, green and red capsicum
1 cm piece of ginger, peeled
2 cm piece of cucumber, seeded
1-2 small chillies or to taste
juice of ¹/₂ lemon and ¹/₂ lime
¹/₂ cup fresh orange juice
2 tablespoons chopped coriander

CRAYFISH

1 uncooked crayfish
1 tablespoon olive oil
salt and pepper
assorted baby salad leaves
1 teaspoon sesame oil

To make salsa, peel mangoes and cut flesh from stone in large pieces. If using canned mango, drain and use juice from mango in salsa but only half the amount of orange juice. Dice first seven ingredients and add to reserved juices. Add coriander. Mix all ingredients and stand to develop flavours. Remove tail from body of crayfish by running a small knife up inside the body of the crayfish to where tail joins. Twist and pull firmly to separate. Split the tail with a sharp knife, leaving the tail joined at fin end. Remove vein. To serve, heat olive oil in a heavy pan until almost smoking. Lightly season crayfish tail with salt and pepper; add to pan flesh side down. The tail should curl around and remain joined at fins.

Cook for 30 seconds to 1 minute. Lightly brown the flesh. Remove tail from pan, place on a tray in a hot oven for 3 minutes. While cooking, toss small amounts of salad leaves in bowl with sesame oil to coat. Arrange in centre of a serving plate. Spoon salsa around outside. Place tail on leaves.

Serves 2-4.

GREEN DOLPHIN RESTAURANT & BAR, KAIKOURA.

POULET FACON BASQUAISE

1 kg chicken meat
2 tablespoons pork fat
250 g tomatoes
6 green capsicums
125 g mushrooms
150 g shoulder bacon
salt and freshly ground pepper
2 cups dry white wine

Cut chicken into 8 serving portions. Brown in pork fat and place to one side. Cut the tomatoes and squeeze out the seeds, and cut the capsicums in little pieces, removing the stems, seeds and white ribs. Cut the mushrooms in half and remove the stalks. Cook the vegetables in pork fat over low heat, stirring for 10 minutes or until the vegetables soften and are lightly browned. Cut the shoulder bacon into fine strips and place in the pan with the chicken. Season with salt and pepper and add the wine. Cover and cook over low heat for 40 minutes, stirring occasionally. Transfer the chicken to a shallow dish. Boil the cooking liquid over high heat until thick. Pour over the chicken and serve immediately. Can be decorated with small Spanish hot peppers. Serves 4.

THE OLD CONVENT, KAIKOURA.

ALWAYS CLOSE TO THE SEA

Kaikoura and the surrounding region are fortunate to have bounty from both sea and land. While blessed with the beauty of the Kaikoura Range and a dramatic rocky shoreline, the region also encloses prosperous agricultural land. In its early days Kaikoura was based on whaling and fishing, and traces of this past lifestyle can still be seen. More recently, Kaikoura entrepreneurs have developed whale, dolphin and bird-watching tours. This emphasis has also led to the participation by New

Zealanders in the collection of information about endangered marine mammal species. It is a great pleasure to take drives along the Kaikoura Peninsula or along the coast road to see the Garden of Memories, the University of Canterbury's field station aquarium, the Kaikoura Lookout or the Takahanga Marae. Other interesting sights include the Kaikoura Coast Track and Fyffe Forest, which contains untouched podocarp forest and many native trees.

Left: Early morning in Kaikoura.
Below: The Crayfish Caravan on the Kaikoura coast offers a 'right-by-the-sea-side' location plus temptingly prepared crays fresh from the sea. A pleasant spot to dunk succulent bits in tartare sauce while you have a look around.
Following pages (144 & 145): Framed by the snowy grandeur of the Southern Alps, Christchurch spreads over the Canterbury Plains.

SMOKED SALMON TARTARE PARCELS

360 g smoked salmon
2 small Spanish onions
2 teaspoons sour cream
2 nips brandy
salt, pepper, chopped dill and chives
2 tablespoons white wine vinegar
1 teaspoon each wasabi paste, and
Dijon mustard
pinch salt, pepper, sugar
½ cup walnut oil
Mesclun leaves
dill sprig
cherry tomatoes to garnish
(about 1 dozen)

Put 24 even slices of smoked salmon to the side. Finely chop the rest of the smoked salmon and mix with 1 chopped Spanish onion, sour cream, brandy and seasonings. (Keep the other for onion rings as a garnish.) Make balls from the mixture. Wrap each ball with 2 slices of salmon and tie with chives. Prepare dressing by mixing together vinegar, wasabi paste, mustard and seasoning using a blender. Gradually add walnut oil and adjust seasoning to taste. Arrange Mesclun leaves in the middle of the serving plate. Place salmon parcels around the leaves. Before serving, sprinkle with walnut dressing and garnish with a sprig of dill, onion rings and cherry tomatoes.
Serves 4 as a starter.

MERCHANTS RESTAURANT,
HOTEL GRAND CHANCELLOR,
CHRISTCHURCH.

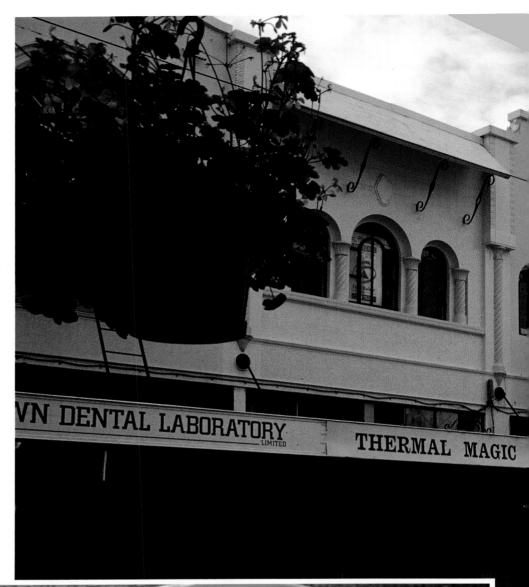

Above: The sunset sky makes an enticing display over Christchurch.

Left: The Christchurch Tram and Arcade. A leisurely way to see the city - just buy a ticket and hop on and off at the tram stops that suit you.

COME TO CHRISTCHURCH

Christchurch - its gardens, its English cosmopolitan air, its university, its theatres and casino, its series of remarkable roadhouses: the Sign of the Kiwi, the Sign of the Bellbird and the Sign of the Takahe - so much to see and enjoy, whether as a tourist or as a resident Cantabrian. For an exhilarating dining experience, ride the Mount Cavendish Gondola up to the summit. There you'll find a restaurant, a multi-media show about the city plus scenic areas where you can ride mountain bikes or paraglide.

GRIMSBY'S STICKY DATE PUDDING

250 g pitted dates, chopped
2 cups boiling water
1/2 teaspoon baking soda
100 g butter
1 cup sugar
3 eggs, beaten
2 cups flour
2 teaspoons baking powder

SAUCE
1 cup golden syrup
1 1/2 cups sugar
1/2 teaspoon salt
125 g butter
1/2 teaspoon vanilla essence
1 cup cream

Soak dates in boiling water and baking soda for half an hour. Cream butter and sugar until fluffy. Add eggs, sifted flour and baking powder. Add dates and liquid. Mix should be wet. Grease a pudding basin, two-thirds fill with mixture and cover with foil. Cook in steamer until firm in centre. Prepare sauce by boiling together all ingredients except vanilla essence and cream. When mixture holds together in a soft ball by testing a sample in cold water, remove from heat and add essence and cream. To serve, flood plate with caramel sauce, spooning some over servings of the warm pudding. Serve with lashings of cream. Serves 6.

GRIMSBY'S RESTAURANT, CHRISTCHURCH.

Lyttelton Harbour. Lying south of Christchurch, the area is rich in military lore and history. Launch trips can be taken to Diamond Harbour or to Quail and Ripapa Islands, which have guided walks over the landscape.

THEY LANDED HERE...

Lyttelton is located on the rugged sides of a very old volcanic crater and is named for Lord Lyttelton, a man who was extremely influential in the establishment of the Church of England colony that founded modern day Lyttelton. Its seafaring background and related memorabilia are on display at the Lyttelton Historical Museum. Lyttelton also has three mid-nineteenth century churches (all built of local stone), that contain a number of interesting historical items and original furnishings. Lyttelton and Christchurch are connected by New Zealand's longest road tunnel, nearly 2 km in length.

SALMON STRIPS SAUTÉED RARE IN HOT NOODLES

800 g fresh salmon fillet, bones removed

200 g noodles or linguine

24 x 2 cm square croutons

SAUCE

100 g palm sugar or jaggery

2 tablespoons Thai fish sauce

6 small hot dried red chillies

2 tablespoons lime juice

2 tablespoons grated root ginger

1 cm fresh ginger, peeled and julienned

1/2 cup chopped coriander

Cut salmon in 2 cm strips. Cook the noodles in well salted water until tender. Drain and rinse under cold water. Set aside. Toast croutons in hot oven until crisp and golden. To make the sauce, cook the palm sugar in heavy-based pot with a little water until a light caramel consistency. Carefully add fish sauce, chillies, lime juice and ginger. Remove from heat and cool. Reheat noodles in the caramel sauce over low heat until well coated. Sauté salmon strips (fleshy side first) in a hot pan, with the ginger and coriander. Turn after 20 seconds and sauté skin side down. To serve, in centre of plate twirl sauced noodles, forming a spiral pattern. Place salmon strips over noodles, forming a lattice. Garnish with chopped coriander and the croutons.
Serves 4.

THE LYTTELTON BRASSERIE, LYTTELTON.

GRIMSBY'S CANTERBURY STYLE BOUILLABAISSE

½ onion, finely sliced
¼ leek, finely sliced lengthwise
4 tomatoes, roughly chopped
2 courgettes, finely diced
1 pinch 'Eight Moon' saffron
(from Rangiora)
1 tablespoon crushed garlic
4 cloves star anise
2 tablespoons each olive oil, Pernod
½ cup white wine
4 cups fish stock
50 g each firm white fish, Akaroa
salmon, fresh squid rings, baby octopus,
crayfish medallions
12 each, king prawns, scallops,
oysters and snails
1 sprig fennel or dill
crusty French bread
mayonnaise with a pinch of saffron
and mixed chilli

This is a traditional French Provençal soup that has been adapted to the local Canterbury market. Scallops, oysters and sandcrabs are borrowed from Nelson, crayfish from the Kaikoura Coast and cod and salmon from Akaroa. This dish is a meal in itself. The key to a good bouillabaisse is the range of seafood. Sauté vegetables, saffron, garlic and anise in olive oil until transparent then add Pernod and flame lightly. Add white wine, stock and larger seafood ie fish and mussels. Simmer for 5 minutes. Add squid, octopus and king prawns. Simmer for 5-7 minutes. To serve, place seafood in dish, pour liquid over and garnish with sprigs of fresh fennel or dill. Toast slices of French bread and spread with saffron mayonnaise, also known as Rouille, pronounced 'Roo wee'.
Serves 4-6.

GRIMSBY'S RESTAURANT, CHRISTCHURCH.

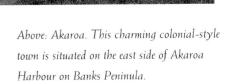

Above: Akaroa. This charming colonial-style town is situated on the east side of Akaroa Harbour on Banks Peninula.

Left: Another dramatic view of Banks Peninsula.

Nice for a Summer Holiday

Timaru is bounded by Patiti Point to the south and the Washdyke Lagoon to the north. The town curves around the beaches of Caroline Bay, which are sought by summer holidaymakers who flock each year to swim and sunbathe or attend the three-week summer carnival there. Caroline Bay also includes parks and gardens to enjoy as well as the relocated wooden lighthouse which was built in 1877. Timaru also has a botanical garden, a large art gallery and the South Canterbury Museum, which contains a number of displays and collections relating to local European and Maori history. Temuka is not far from Timaru - just a few kilometres north where the Opihi River flows into the sea. In Temuka sportsmen can easily find pleasant tree-shaded river banks where salmon and trout can be caught - later to be fried, baked or grilled as the main course of a delicious gourmet meal.

Old shed on a paddock near Timaru.

TURKEY SUMMER SALAD

1 small turkey breast
1 cinnamon quill
6 whole peppercorns
2 oranges
2 bay leaves
2 whole cloves
1 bunch young spinach
1 sprig fresh coriander
1 red onion
1 orange

DRESSING

¹/₂ cup olive oil
juice of ¹/₂ orange
1 tablespoon wholegrain mustard
4 tablespoons cider vinegar
freshly ground black pepper
and salt
1 teaspoon Manuka honey

Place turkey breast and next five ingredients into a saucepan and add enough cold water to cover turkey breast. Gently poach until turkey is cooked, approximately 30-40 minutes. Cool turkey in cooking liquid. Remove turkey and slice very thinly and place on a plate. Wash spinach and coriander, removing any coarse spinach stems. Slice onion finely and segment the orange. Arrange ingredients on turkey slices. Make dressing by combining all ingredients. Drizzle on and around turkey and salad. Arrange some coriander sprigs and orange peel knots around salad for decoration. Serves 4.

GINGER & GARLIC LICENSED
RESTAURANT, TIMARU.

CENTRAL OTAGO & FIORDLAND

THERE ARE ENOUGH HOLIDAY DESTINATIONS in Central Otago and Fiordland for even the most enthusiastic jetsetter. Sweeping harbours, endless rugged mountains, coastal bays and lakes - all offer their unique beauty. One famous scene is shown here: the splendour of Mitre Peak reflected in the Milford Sound. For this part of our journey, we started near the Haast Pass and drove east to Lake Wanaka to sample food from Wanaka's superb restaurants. We tried tender rack of lamb garnished with couscous and savoured a most glamourous Grand Marnier cheesecake drizzled with creamy white and dark chocolate. Next, we visited Arrowtown and then Queenstown, where you can re-explore the historic gold fields, ride a gondola ferry to the restaurant high on Bob's Peak or jetboat down the Shotover River. The prime slopes near Queenstown draw winter sports lovers to the snow for breathtaking skiing and all the fun a resort can offer. From Queenstown we bring you medallion of wild boar with chicken breast and Applewood Cheddar. After that, it was on to Clyde, where we found a moist, incredibly good carrot cake topped with orangy cream-cheese icing.

WHITE CHOCOLATE & GRAND MARNIER CHEESECAKE

CRUST
1 cup biscuit crumbs
200 g butter, melted
1 teaspoon finely grated lemon zest

CHEESECAKE
160 g white chocolate
¾ cup white sugar
750 g cream cheese
2 large eggs
1 teaspoon finely grated lemon zest
1½ tablespoons lemon juice
2 teaspoons vanilla essence
1 tablespoon Grand Marnier
4 large egg whites

To make the crust, first pre-heat oven to 180°C. Combine all crust ingredients and press into a 20-22 cm cake tin lined with baking paper and sides brushed with butter. Bake for 5 minutes until lightly browned. To make filling, melt chocolate slowly over double boiler, stirring occasionally to avoid over-cooking. Place half the sugar, cream cheese, eggs and lemon zest in mixer on high

AIRSHOWS & ADVENTURING

Above is Lake Wanaka, which borders Haast Pass. This lovely lake near the Harris Mountains is fed by the Matukituki River. The township of Wanaka looks north up the lake, which is bordered by willows and poplars whose rustling leaves exhibit a golden beauty in the autumn season. The Mount Aspiring National Park Headquarters is located in Wanaka. From there visitors are guided to the best places for their particular pursuits. Skiers find their way to the Treble Cone and Mount

speed for 5-6 minutes until light and fluffy. Add lemon juice, vanilla essence, Grand Marnier and continue beating. Transfer mix to another bowl and fold in white chocolate. In a clean bowl, beat egg whites to soft peaks and add remaining sugar. Beat until all sugar is dissolved. Fold egg white mixture into cream cheese mixture and turn out into pie crust. Smooth over top and bake. Bake for 10 minutes at 180°C then 50-55 minutes at 110°C.

WHITE CHOCOLATE SAUCE

80 g white chocolate melts
¼ cup cream
boiling water to mix

Melt chocolate in double boiler over medium heat, add cream and warm over low heat. Mix well so all the chocolate is dissolved. Add boiling water and mix to a smooth sauce.

DARK CHOCOLATE SAUCE

80 g dark cooking chocolate
boiling water

Melt chocolate in double boiler over medium heat and gradually stir in boiling water until smooth.
Leave cake in tin until cold and refrigerate overnight. Cut into slices and drizzle with white and dark chocolate sauces. Add whipped cream and fruit.
Chocolate sauces can be left in refrigerator and warmed to soften again when required.
Serves 6-8.

CAPRICCIO RESTAURANT, WANAKA.

Cadrona skifields and anglers to the many rivers in the locale. There is also a nordic ski area at Waiorau as well as opportunities for heli-skiing and ice skating. Walkers have too many choices to mention them all: from trips to lakeshores such as the walk to Lake Hawea to those with a lofty viewpoint, such as the track up to Mount Roy. Mountaineers and rock climbers find exhilarating climbs in the alpine areas. The Wanaka environs are heaven for the adventurous, with every sort of mountaineering available; with rafting, canoeing, gliding and paragliding; plus hunting and fishing excursions as well as horse trekking and scenic flights. Wanaka also hosts the yearly Warbirds over Wanaka Airshow, attended by aviation history buffs from all over the world.

FRENCH RACK OF LAMB WITH FRENCH BEANS, COUSCOUS & RED CAPSICUM AIOLI

HERB CRUST
5 slices white toast bread
4 tablespoons chopped parsley
1 teaspoon chopped rosemary
2 teaspoons chopped garlic
1 tablespoon whole grain mustard
salt and pepper
200 g butter, melted

LAMB
4 x 250 g French lamb racks
salt and pepper

AIOLI
1 large red capsicum
oil
1/2 cup each yoghurt, sour cream
1 teaspoon each finely chopped garlic,
mint

COUSCOUS
120 g couscous
knob of butter

2 cups reduced lamb or beef stock (jus)
120 g French beans, blanched
sprig of mint to garnish

To make herb crust, place bread in food processor on high until bread is crumbed. Add parsley, rosemary, garlic, mustard, and salt and pepper. Slowly pour in the butter. To prepare lamb, seal off racks by quickly cooking all sides for a few seconds and lightly season meat with salt and pepper. Place herb crust mixture on top of meat to form a thin crust and bake in oven for 15-20 minutes at 190°C.

To make the red capsicum aioli, brush capsicum with oil and bake in a medium oven until covered in blisters. Quickly drop into cold water and then peel the skin away, removing core and seeds from the centre. Place into food processor until smooth. Add yoghurt, sour cream, chopped garlic and mint. To prepare the couscous, lightly steam couscous, adding a knob of butter and season with salt and pepper. Place 4 large mounds of couscous on a baking tray and flatten slightly. Top with the aioli and bake for 5 minutes until just starting to brown.

Heat lamb jus and add blanched beans into jus.

To assemble, place beans and jus in centre of plates and place couscous on plate with metal slice. Place lamb racks (which have been rested for a few minutes after removing from oven) on plate and garnish with a sprig of mint.

Serves 4.

CAPRICCIO RESTAURANT, WANAKA.

WHERE THE RIVER MEETS THE SEA

*Cold smoked salmon and eel with
asparagus and tartare sauce
3 asparagus spears
3 pieces smoked salmon
3 slices smoked eel*

**Cook asparagus on high power in
microwave until just tender for about
1 minute. Put smoked salmon on
board, place smoked eel on top of
salmon, and roll around each
asparagus spear. Cut in half and
arrange around a bowl of
tartare sauce.**

TARTARE SAUCE
*3 tablespoons mayonnaise
1 tablespoon each, chopped gherkins,
chopped olives,
chopped chives*

**Mix all ingredients together.
Serves 1.**

RIPPLES RESTAURANT, WANAKA.

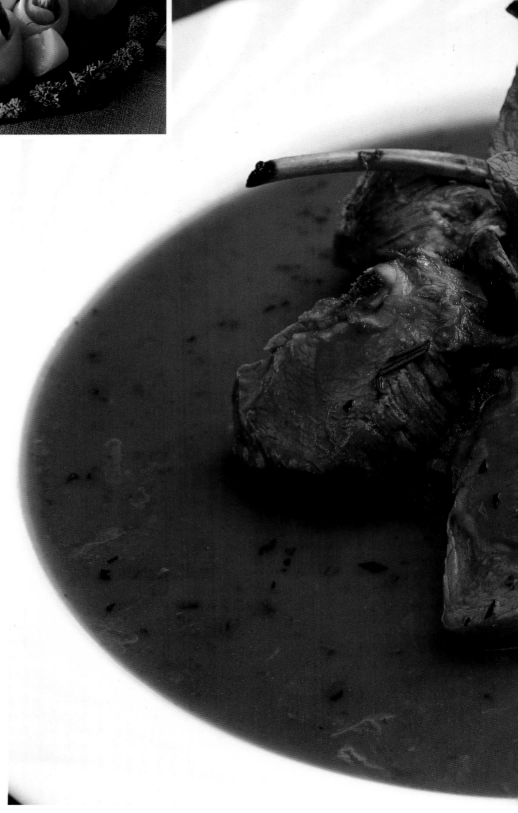

RACK OF LAMB WITH MINTED PEA PÂTÉ ON A ROSEMARY JUS

MINTED PEA PÂTÉ

500 g minted peas, cooked
1 teaspoon crushed garlic
salt and pepper
1 teaspoon lemon juice

LAMB

4 racks of lamb
1 tablespoon olive oil
2 cups red wine
freshly ground black pepper and salt
chopped rosemary
fresh mint
sprig of rosemary

To make pâté, place all ingredients in food processor and blend until puréed.

Season lamb racks and seal in hot pan with olive oil. Cover rib bones in foil to prevent charring. Place in moderate oven for approximately 15 minutes. Remove racks from pan. Deglaze pan with red wine. Add pepper, salt and chopped rosemary and reduce by half.

To serve, place minted pea pâté in centre of plate. Arrange lamb rack around pâté.

Pour rosemary jus over rack.

Garnish with fresh mint and a sprig of rosemary.

Serves 4.

THE STABLES RESTAURANT & WINE BAR, ARROWTOWN.

164

SWISS CHOCOLATE DACQUOISE ON A FLOWING SEA OF RASPBERRY & CHOCOLATE

MERINGUES

4 egg whites

¾ cup sugar

CHOCOLATE MOUSSE

325 g dark chocolate

1 cup cream

1 teaspoon powdered gelatine

2 tablespoons water

2 eggs, separated

¼ cup Grand Marnier

1¼ cups cream, lightly whipped

RASPBERRY COULIS

250 g raspberries

¾ cup icing sugar

CHOCOLATE SAUCE

1¼ cups water

½ cup sugar

250 g dark chocolate, chopped

1 tablespoon brandy

GARNISH

3 strawberries

cocoa powder

sprigs of mint

flowers

To make meringues, place egg whites in mixer and whip until peaks form. Gradually add sugar until well blended. Place meringue mixture in piping bag and pipe 5 cm rounds onto a greased oven tray. This should yield 12 individual meringues. Place in oven for 2 hours at 90-100°C. To make the chocolate mousse, melt chocolate and 1 cup cream in a double pan, whisking constantly. Dissolve gelatine in water. Add egg yolks, liqueur and dissolved gelatine.

FIND THE PAST - TODAY!

Follow Highway 6 northeast out of Queenstown, and you will soon find Arrowtown, which is pleasantly situated on the Arrow River. Gold from the river built the town and gold still hides under the Arrow's flowing waters - enough to keep weekend prospectors busy fishing sparkling flakes from the last swirl of sand in their gold pans.

Fold in lightly whipped cream. Then fold in lightly whipped egg white. Refrigerate for 4 hours. To make raspberry coulis, blend ingredients together and pass through sieve to remove seeds.

To make chocolate sauce, place water and sugar in a pan and bring to boil. Remove from heat. Add chopped chocolate and whisk until melted. Add brandy and whisk until blended. Refrigerate for 1 hour.

To assemble dacquoise, cover half a large plate with raspberry coulis and the other half with chocolate sauce. Place meringue in centre. Pipe with mousse. Place a second meringue on top and repeat. Then place a third meringue on top. Garnish with strawberries and dust with cocoa powder, then top with a sprig of mint and a flower.

Serves 4.

THE STABLES RESTAURANT & WINE BAR, ARROWTOWN.

Arrowtown has preserved the charm of its historic past while offering up-to-date amenities and amusements for the ever-growing numbers of tourists who visit here each year to see Miner's Monument, the Lakes District Centennial Museum, Tobin's Track or to wander through Macetown, 15km upriver. Now a quiet ghost town, Macetown once bustled with miners manning the machines that crushed gold-bearing quartz rock to extract its ore.

MEDALLION OF WILD BOAR

¼ chicken breast, chopped
1 clove garlic, crushed
2 leaves green sage
15 g Applewood Cheddar
4 cups plain flour
8 egg yolks
3 whole eggs
1 tablespoon salt
1 tablespoon oil
50 g medallion of wild boar
1 teaspoon apricot mustard
2 shallots, diced (or red onion if shallots unavailable)
1 teaspoon chopped pistachios
2 teaspoons redcurrant jelly
2 tablespoons orange juice
2 teaspoons pickled ginger juice
1 teaspoon fresh lime juice
white wine
paprika to garnish
herb garnish

Season chicken with garlic, green sage, Applewood Cheddar. To make pasta, place flour, egg yolks, salt and oil in food processor and blend. Immediately wrap in plastic film as discolouration will occur within 20 minutes. Put in refrigerator to rest. Roll out pasta, working quickly to prevent the pasta from drying out. Roll through each setting on pasta machine until the lowest setting is achieved and the pasta becomes transparent. Cover with a damp cloth immediately. Cut rounds of pasta. Place cheddar mixture into centre of rounds and fold into crescent shape.

Smear top of boar medallion with
apricot mustard, shallots, pistachios.
Seal on the bottom of meat only and
place on finely cut root vegetables.
Spread with butter and place in oven.
When cooked rare, rest for
2 minutes. Reduce redcurrant jelly
and orange juice by half. Season with
lime and ginger juice. Correct
consistency with white wine. Blanch
pasta and then pan fry and dust
with paprika.
Serves 1

CLANCY'S RESTAURANT,
LAKELAND HOTEL, QUEENSTOWN.

*Breathtaking aerial view of the approach
to Queenstown, Lake Wakatipu and
the Remarkables.*

SEARGRILLED SALMON ESCALOPE

700 g boneless salmon escalope
with skin on
¼ cup each flour, olive oil,
chopped fresh herbs
8 shallots, chopped
2 cloves garlic, finely chopped
1 cup balsamic vinegar
1 cup red wine
2 tablespoons sugar
80 g smoked crayfish medallions
1½ cup mashed potato
2 teaspoons chopped fresh tarragon
½ cup Beurre Blanc
salt and pepper

Heat chargrill or grill to high.
Lightly flour salmon before dredging
through olive oil and fresh herbs.
Grill for 30 seconds skin side up.
Place in pre-heated 180°C oven for 4
minutes then rest in warm place.
Dry roast shallots and garlic in hot
pan, add balsamic vinegar, red
wine, sugar and reduce until a
syrup is formed.
Combine crayfish with mashed
potato, seasonings, add
tarragon and warm through.
Spoon onto a plate drizzled
with Beurre Blanc and
balsamic reduction.
Garnish with mizuna or
rocket greens.
Use a fish slice to separate
skin from salmon, place salmon
on top of mash and use crisp
skin as a garnish.
Serves 4.

BOARDWALK SEAFOOD
RESTAURANT, QUEENSTOWN.

Above: Jet boating in Queenstown - only one of many sports to enjoy here. Queenstown also offers scenic walks, boat tours of Lake Wakatipu and round trips to Arrowtown in four-wheel drive vehicles.

Left: Reminiscent of Mexico or the North American southwest - an adobe house built in Queenstown.

A RESORT OF DISTINCTION

Queenstown: truly a unique resort community of distinction with its awe-inspiring lakeside setting and mountains sternly guarding every direction. The Coronet Peak ski field to the north and the Remarkables ski fields east of Queenstown are recreation areas enhanced with full facilities for the enjoyment of sportspeople. Lifts, restaurants, ski instruction, and - for the over-the-top adventurous - wilderness skiing accessible by helicopter. This holiday town has other attractions too, such as the Queenstown Underwater World, the Skyline Gondola and Restaurant, the Queenstown Motor Museum, historic Eichardt's Hotel, Winkys Goldfield Museum and the Kiwi and Birdlife Park.

CARROT CAKE

3 eggs

1 cup each brown sugar,

raw sugar

¾ cup oil

2 teaspoons vanilla essence

2 cups wholemeal flour

½ teaspoon salt

2 teaspoons each baking soda,

ground cinnamon

1 teaspoon ground nutmeg

¼ cup milk

3 cups grated carrot

1 cup desiccated coconut

½ cup chopped walnuts

225 g tin crushed pineapple, drained

ICING (optional)

50 g butter

1 teaspoon grated orange rind

¼ cup cream cheese

½ teaspoon vanilla

1 cup icing sugar

1-2 tablespoons orange juice

Beat eggs, add sugars, oil and vanilla and beat well. Mix together flour, salt, baking soda, spices and fold into egg mixture. Add milk, carrot, coconut, walnuts and pineapple. Stir gently but thoroughly. Put in greased and floured 23-cm, round tin. Bake at 180°C for approximately 1½ hours. Leave in the tin for awhile before turning out. To prepare the icing, cream together butter and cream cheese, add vanilla, orange rind and icing sugar. Stir in enough orange juice to make it smooth and creamy. Spread over top and sides of cake.

OLIVERS RESTAURANT AND
LODGE, CLYDE,
CENTRAL OTAGO.

It's easy to see why Olivers Restaurant has won national acclaim. Built in 1874 of stone quarried from the Cromwell Gorge, its atmosphere is unhurried and traditional. It's a place to relax and enjoy fabulous cuisine like the luscious carrot cake pictured here, and to look around and appreciate the added enhancements like beautifully presented jars of homemade fruit and jam.

Left: Lake Te Anau, a gateway to Fiordland.

Below: A long lingering look down a curve of the Doubtful Sound. One of the deep, glacier-carved channels cutting into Fiordland National Park, the sound is not completely cut off for those who would like to experience its spectacular reaches. Launch trips cruise this steep-sided inlet, and a road from Deep Cove links the Doubtful Sound with Lake Manapouri.

OTAGO & SOUTHLAND

OTAGO AND SOUTHLAND are east of Mt Aspiring National Park and south of the Canterbury Plains. Oamaru, known for splendid stone architecture, is north of Dunedin, a city made prosperous by the Otago gold boom. We began this trek in Oamaru, where we struck a rich lode of tangy chicken heaped with berry-fruit sauce and stuffed with local Brie cheese and Otago apricots! Just as lucky in Dunedin, we found a dark chocolate pudding with rich-as-can-be banana caramel sauce and a super-good sourdough recipe that makes a loaf so delicious it will vanish before it has cooled. As we travelled in Otago and Southland, we found the seafood fresh and tasty – the heart of many good meals. Bluff, the southernmost town in the South Island, has its oyster season. And what a season! People wait all year to taste them. We found an Invercargill restaurant that uses Bluff oysters to perfection in a grilled-oyster salad with balsamic dressing. The Southern Scenic Route and the beautiful Catlin Forest are not far from here, and a Catlin scene appears on these two pages. We never went hungry with mouth-watering meat, poultry and seafood wherever we went. Add local produce, freshly baked breads, scones and shortbreads – a wonderful variety of tastes to savour!

Below: Oamaru, centre of a lush sheep-farming area, is renowned for its striking stone architecture.

Breast of Chicken Filled With Apricot & Brie Cheese, Served With a Tangy Berry Fruit Sauce

TANGY BERRY FRUIT SAUCE

100 g each raspberries, blackberries, boysenberries
1 cup caster sugar
1¼ cups Madeira Port

1 chicken supreme
1 apricot, pitted
Brie cheese, two slices

Cook berries, sugar and port together and strain. Fill chicken with apricot and Brie cheese. Seal in a hot frypan with a little oil. Bake in oven for 12-15 minutes at 190°C. Place a little sauce on garnished plate, slice chicken in three, place on top of sauce, trickle more sauce on top of chicken. Serve with fresh side salad.

LAST POST RESTAURANT,
OAMARU, SOUTHLAND.

CADBURY'S CHOCOLATE PUDDING WITH BANANA & CARAMEL SAUCE

PUDDING

100 g each butter, sugar

2 eggs

100 g flour

2 tablespoons Cadbury's Cocoa Powder

1 teaspoon baking powder

50 g Cadbury's Chocolate Buttons

CARAMEL & BANANA SAUCE

200 g caster sugar

200 g cream

1 banana

Mix butter and sugar, add the eggs, gradually mix in the flour, cocoa, baking powder and chocolate buttons. Place 3 tablespoons of the mixture into a buttered and floured ramekin. Cook in the microwave for 1 minute or until set, but not too firm. Repeat with remaining mixture. Note: Microwaves vary in power so experiment with your own to find the right time for your appliance.

To make the sauce, caramelise sugar, then gradually add warm cream to avoid overflowing. Add sliced banana.

Serves 4-6.

NINETY FIVE, DUNEDIN.

JUTLAND CHICKEN

4 boneless chicken breasts

FILLING
500 g ham ends
¹/₂ cup dried apricots
2 medium onions
100 g cream cheese
large splash of green ginger wine
seasoning to taste
4 slices mozzarella cheese
oil
handful of seeds - eg sesame or
poppy seeds

SAUCE
500 ml apricot pulp
1 tablespoon brown sugar
rum to taste

Make a pocket in each chicken breast. Blend all filling ingredients except mozzarella, oil and seeds in food processor. Consistency needs to be stiff. Place a spoonful of filling into each chicken breast. Place a slice of mozzarella on top. Fold flap of each breast back over the top. Oil a pan or baking dish and put breasts in dish. Allow plenty of space between each breast. Brush breasts with oil and sprinkle with seeds. Bake at 220-250°C for about 20-25 minutes or until cooked. To make the sauce, heat pulp and brown sugar until sugar is dissolved. Add rum to taste. Place cooked breast on plate and pour sauce over and around it. Serves 4.

PALMS CAFÉ, DUNEDIN.

Right: A view over the city of Dunedin.

MIXED GRAIN SOURDOUGH

THE DAY BEFORE BAKING

Feed the sourdough starter: Add 200 g wholemeal flour and 2 cups lukewarm filtered water to 500 ml sourdough starter* (* a wholemeal and water ferment). Allow to ferment overnight in a covered, but ventilated glass container, at room temperature. Soak together in 250 ml filtered water: 4 tablespoons each kibbled wheat, coarse cornmeal, rolled oats, linseed.

THE DAY OF CREATION

Reserve 2 cups of starter for next day's baking. To the remaining 700 ml of starter, whisk in 100 ml of lukewarm filtered water, add soaked grain, 1 teaspoon of sea salt and 750 g of wholemeal flour. Knead to form a dough, correcting consistency with additional water or flour. Knead for 10 minutes, until dough is smooth and springs back when indented.

Lightly oil with cold-pressed canola oil, mist with water and prove until a third risen, (up to 1 ½ hours depending on how active the starter is), then rest for 10 minutes at room temperature. Shape into 2 loaves. Prove loaves until they 'bloom' up in tins, 1½ hours. Bake for 1 hour in a medium/hot oven until bottom of loaf is golden. Good eating!

If you have difficulty in obtaining the starter, Tangenté can supply.

Makes 2 loaves.

TANGENTÉ BAKERY & CAFÉ, DUNEDIN.

Left: Larnach Castle, one of Dunedin's most well known examples of Scottish architecture. Built in 1871, it is furnished with Venetian glass and early New Zealand furniture and its impressive entry stairs have stone lions. Larnach Castle also has a hanging staircase, battlements 300 metres above the sea and extensive grounds.

Dunedin has over twenty buildings of great historic importance and is known for fine Victorian architecture and well-appointed gardens.

PARSLEY & PINE NUT PESTO

250 g bunch of parsley
50 g Parmesan cheese, grated
50 g lightly toasted pine nuts
½ teaspoon sea salt
3 tablespoons cold-pressed canola oil
1 tablespoon crushed garlic

Remove the parsley tops from any stalks. Place all ingredients into food processor and blend to a smooth paste. Correct consistency with oil and taste for salt. Use on pasta, breads or in dressings. Makes about ¾ cup.

TANGENTÉ BAKERY & CAFÉ, DUNEDIN.

CHARMS OF THE CATLINS

The Catlins district is about 100 kilometres southwest of Dunedin and is just south of Balclutha. The town of Owaka is considered its centre, and the Owaka reserves are prized for their rugged beaches, native bush, waterfalls and sea caves. One interesting sight is Curio Bay, which is a fossilised forest floor, and another is Catlins Lake, which is actually a tidal river about 8 kilometres upstream from the sea. The lake is stocked with sea-run trout at certain times and is also a favourite of boaties, yachties and duckshooters. Nearby the lake are Cathedral Caves. Well worth a visit, the caves are only accessible during the two hours around low tide.

Left: The photo left shows a many-tiered waterfall in the Catlins Forest Park area. The park has many walkways and a variety of waterfalls to view, including Barr, Wilkes, Purakaunui and Matai Falls.

PALMS-STYLE FISH OMELET

oil
400 g fish fillets
flour
4 eggs
1 tablespoon grated cheese
2 teaspoons assorted seeds (eg pumpkin,
poppy, sesame)
2 teaspoons Parmesan cheese

Heat medium omelet pan and oil base and sides well. Dust fillets in flour. Beat eggs until thick. Place fillets in egg mix and spread in pan. It is best to have fillets contact bottom of the pan or the top layers will be slow to cook. Pour remaining mix over and around. Sprinkle top with cheese, seeds, and Parmesan. Bake in oven at 200-250°C until set and golden brown, about 10-12 minutes. To remove from pan run a flexible slice all around and under to free sticky bits. Take pan to a warm plate. Tilt over plate and slide omelet onto plate with the aid of the slice. Serves 2.

For more servings, increase ingredients proportionally and use a bigger pan. The bigger the omelet, the more difficult it is to remove in one piece.

PALMS CAFÉ, DUNEDIN.

Right: A striking example of the architecture for which Invercargill is famous.

MUTTONBIRD IN TARRAGON & FENNEL SAUCE

4 muttonbirds
1 small onion, sliced
½ teaspoon crushed garlic
1 tablespoon oil
½ cup dry white wine
4 stalks fresh tarragon
2 teaspoons fennel seeds
200 ml cream

Simmer muttonbirds on low heat for 2-3 hours. Discard fat, remove legs and breast meat. Sauté onion and garlic in oil. Add wine in pan with tarragon and fennel seeds and reduce by half. Remove tarragon and add cream, muttonbird breast and legs. Simmer to reduce to good consistency. Excellent served with a kumara and pickled ginger salad. Serves 2-4.

GERRARDS RESTAURANT,
INVERCARGILL, SOUTHLAND.

GRILLED BLUFF OYSTER SALAD

3-4 bluff oysters
2 slices each roasted green and
red capsicums
1 slice mozzarella cheese
salad greens, including purple
basil if available
2 marinated Kalamata olives

DRESSING
1 tablespoon balsamic vinegar
¼ cup virgin olive oil
½ small clove garlic, crushed
1 tablespoon capers

Wrap oysters in capsicum with a small slice of mozzarella. Grill for about 3-4 minutes, until oysters are warm and cheese is melted. To make the dressing, slowly pour oil over vinegar and garlic in food processor. Pulse in capers when dressing is desired consistency. Place oysters on top of salad and drizzle over dressing. Add olives. Serve with freshly ground pepper. Serves 1.

GERRARDS RESTAURANT,
INVERCARGILL,
SOUTHLAND.

SUCCULENT SOUTHERN SEAFOOD

Just 27 kilometres south of Invercargill, the major port of Bluff faces Foveaux Strait and Stewart Island. Bluff is home to the Foveaux Strait oyster, known as Tio para by the Maori, and more commonly called the Bluff oyster. Bluff holds its Oyster Festival in April, about a month after the

oyster season begins. The Paua House with its display of beautiful greeny blue shells is a reminder of other succulent seafood available here. After a walk up Bluff Hill to view Tiwai Point, the Awarua Lagoon, the Foveaux Strait, Toetoes Bay, Dog Island and Ruapuke Island, what could be better than looking forward to a meal of paua fritters, grilled oysters, sautéed muttonbird, savoury lobster, salmon fillets or perfectly prepared mussels?

Bluff is a fishing town, and the photo above shows fishing boats at rest in the harbour, awaiting the next voyage out to sea.

WEIGHTS AND MEASURES

The recipes in this book are adapted from original recipes. They have been tested by the chefs who created them and by appreciative diners who enjoyed them. For best results when you prepare the recipes, use standard metric measures (250 ml cup, 15 ml tablespoon and 5 ml teaspoon) unless otherwise stated. *

Follow recipe instructions carefully, use level measurements and follow the specified cooking times. (The oven-temperature table below is a guide only. For best accuracy, refer to your own cooker instruction book.)

* In NZ, USA and UK, 1 tablespoon = 15 ml.
  In Australia 1 tablespoon = 20 ml.

OVEN SETTING EQUIVALENTS (TO NEAREST 10°C)

Description	Fahrenheit	Celsius	Gas regulo No
Very cool	225 - 275	110 - 140	1/4 - 1
Cool	300 - 325	150 - 160	2 - 3
Moderate	350 - 375	180 - 190	4 - 5
Hot	400 - 450	200 - 230	6 - 8
Very hot	475 - 500	250 - 260	9 - 10

Grams to Ounces: These are converted to the nearest round number.

GRAMS	OUNCES	GRAMS	OUNCES	GRAMS	OUNCES
25	= 1	175	= 6	325	= 11
50	= 2	200	= 7	350	= 12
75	= 3	225	= 8	375	= 13
100	= 3.5	250	= 9	400	= 14
125	= 4	275	= 10	425	= 15
150	= 5	300	= 10.5	450	= 16

1 kilogram = 1000 grams = 2 lb 4 oz

Short Glossary

The following is a short glossary of some cooking terms used in this book.

Béarnaise sauce: A French classic. Vinegar, wine, tarragon and shallots are reduced together and then finished with egg yolks and butter. For meat, fish, eggs and vegetables.

Compote: Fresh or dried fruit cooked in syrup. Sometimes flavoured with liquor or spices.

Coulis: Thick purée or sauce. Can be made from a variety of ingredients.

Couscous: Cooked granular semolina or steamed cracked wheat. Can also refer to a Middle Eastern dish that combines semolina or cracked wheat with lamb, chickpeas and vegetables.

Coverture chocolate: Professional-quality coating chocolate. Has a high gloss and forms a thinner coating than ordinary confectionery coatings.

Cumberland sauce: Of English origin. Traditionally contains redcurrant jelly, port, orange and lemon zests, mustard and other seasonings. Used for poultry and game.

Dacquoise: Round, sometimes nut-flavoured meringues which are stacked and filled with whipped cream or buttercream. Can be served chilled with fruit.

Deglaze: To add stock or liquor to a frypan after food and excess fat are removed so that browned bits can be loosened and then mixed with other ingredients to make a sauce base.

Mesclun: Also called salad mix. A potpourri of tender salad greens.

Mirepoix: A mix of diced vegetables and herbs sautéed in butter. Can be a seasoning or a bed on which foods are braised.

Risotto: Italian dish made by adding hot stock to rice as it cooks. Liquid is added just when rice has absorbed all the original liquid. Makes creamy rice with grains that remain separate.

Rösti: Swiss term meaning golden crisp.

Roulade: A thin meat slice rolled around a bread, vegetable, cheese or meat filling.

Tapenade: A thick paste of capers, anchovies, black olives, olive oil, lemon juice, seasonings and occasionally tuna. From Provence.

White chocolate: Mixture of sugar, cocoa butter, milk solids, lecithin and vanilla without chocolate liquor.

Zest: The coloured part of fresh citrus peel. Contains the aromatic oils that lend flavour to food.

Note: The recipes in this book are original creations. In some cases the classic methods have been changed to suit the chef's style.

PHOTOGRAPHIC & ILLUSTRATION CREDITS

All photographs by Ian Baker except;

John Cobb/Penguin Books: 12-13, 14-15, 55 (insert).
108-109, 122-123 (insert),124-125, 132-133, 152-153,
156-157, 158-159, 169, 172-173, 174-175, 182, 184,
188-189, 190-191, 194-195.

Fiordland Travel: 173.

Doc Ross: 167.

Tourism Taranaki: 52-53.

Tourism Waikato: 62-63.

Pauline Whimp: 11 (map).

Tranz/Joan Willis: 34-35, 36-37, 50-51, 66-67.

Visual Impact: 24-25, 26-27, 74-75, 80-81, 106-107,
138-139, 144-145, 166-167, 180-181.

RESTAURANT GUIDE

NORTHLAND & AUCKLAND

ATOMIC CAFÉ, 121 Ponsonby Road, Ponsonby, Auckland, ph 09 376 4954

BISTRO 40, 40 Marsden Road, Paihia, Bay of Islands, ph 09 402 7444

CIN CIN ON QUAY, 99 Quay Street, Auckland, ph 09 307 6966

ESSENCE, 70-72 Jervois Road, Herne Bay, Auckland, ph 09 376 2049

GERHARD'S RESTAURANT & BAR, 572 Great North Road, Grey Lynn, Auckland, ph 09 320 1705

KERMADEC RESTAURANT, Level 1, cnr Lower Hobson & Quay Streets, Auckland, ph 09 309 0412

NAUTILUS RESTAURANT, Gulf Harbour Village, Whangaparaoa, Auckland, ph 09 424 3549

STANMORE COTTAGE RESTAURANT, 201 Brightside Road, Stanmore Bay, Whangaparaoa, Auckland, ph 09 424 7074

COROMANDEL, BAY OF PLENTY & EAST CAPE

BRIAN BORU HOTEL, 200 Richmond Street, Thames, ph 07 868 6523

KESSALLS RESTAURANT & BAR, Shop 3, The Village Centre, Jubilee Drive, Pauanui, ph 07 864 8825

PUKA PARK LODGE RESTAURANT, Mount Avenue, Pauanui Beach, ph 07 864 8088

RUMOURS RESTAURANT, 81 Pukuatua Street, Rotorua, ph 07 347 7277

SHELLS RESTAURANT & BAR, 119 Pepe Road, Tairua Beach, ph 07 864 7540

SOMERSET COTTAGE, 30 Bethlehem Road, Bethlehem, Tauranga, ph 07 576 6889

TARANAKI, KING COUNTRY & WAIKATO

LEFT BANK INTERNATIONAL RESTAURANT & BAR, Marlborough Place, Hamilton, ph 07 839 3354

REPLETE CAFÉ/DELI & CATERING CONSULTANCY, 45 Heu Heu Street, Taupo, ph 07 378 0606

THE RUAPEHU ROOM, The Grant Chateau, Mt Ruapehu, Tongariro National Park, ph 07 892 3809

RUSTICI BRASSERIE, 312 Victoria Street, Riverbank Mall, Hamilton, ph 07 839 1111

WAIRARAPA & HAWKE'S BAY

ANATOLES CAFÉ, 12 Browning Street, Napier, ph 06 835 7800

AYLSTONE, Private Lodgings, Wine Library & Larder, Huangarua Road, Martinborough, ph 06 306 9505

BAYSWATER ON THE BEACH, 5 Harding Road, Ahuriri, Napier, ph 06 835 8517

THE MARTINBOROUGH BISTROT, Martinborough Hotel, The Square, Martinborough, ph 06 306 9350

PIERRE SUR LE QUAI, 62 West Quay, Ahuriri, Napier, ph 06 834 0189

TOADS LANDING, Windover Gardens, Homebush, Masterton, ph 06 377 3793

VIDAL WINERY BRASSERIE, 913 Aubyns Street East, Hastings, ph 06 876 8105

MANAWATU & WELLINGTON

THE BATHHOUSE CAFÉ & BAR, 161 Broadway Avenue, Palmerston North, ph 06 355 0051

BOULCOTT STREET BISTRO, Plimmer House, 99 Boulcott Street, Wellington, ph 04 499 4199

CAFÉ VAVASSEUR, 201 Broadway Avenue, Palmerston North, ph 06 359 3167

COUNTRY LIFE RESTAURANT, Main Road, Waikanae, ph 04 293 6353

IL CASINO RISTORANTE, 108-112 Tory Street, Wellington, ph 04 385 7496

LOGAN BROWN, 192 Cuba Street, Wellington, ph 04 801 5114

MICHAEL'S RESTAURANT, 281 Wickstead Street, Wanganui, ph 06 345 2690

RUTH PRETTY CATERING & COOKING SCHOOL, 41 School Road, Te Horo, ph 06 364 3161

MARLBOROUGH & NELSON

AN EPICUREAN AFFAIR, Stone Aerie Estate, Dog Point Road, Blenheim, ph 03 572 9639

BOAT SHED CAFÉ, 350 Wakefield Quay, Nelson, ph 03 546 9783

GOTHIC GOURMET LICENSED RESTAURANT & TAVERN, 208 High Street, Motueka, ph 03 528 6699

HOTEL D'URVILLE, 52 Queen Street, Blenheim, ph 03 577 9945

JESTER HOUSE CAFÉ, Coastal Highway, Tasman, ph 03 526 6742

KORURANGI CAFÉ, Korurangi Farm, Lansdowne Road, Richmond, Nelson, ph 03 544 6500

THE DARLING DILL CAFÉ, cnr Main Road & Neil Street, Havelock, Marlborough, ph 03 574 2844

WEST COAST

THE BAY HOUSE CAFÉ, Beach Road, Tauranga Bay, Cape Foulwind, Westport, ph 03 789 7133

BEECHWOODS, State Highway 6, Murchison, ph 03 523 9993

DIEGO'S RESTAURANT & BAR, 18 Wakefield Street, Westport, ph 03 789 7640

LAKE PARINGA CAFÉ, Main Road, State Highway 6, Lake Paringa, South Westland, ph 03 751 0110

TRAPPER'S RESTAURANT, 79 Revell Street, Hokitika, ph 03 755 5133

KAIKOURA & CANTERBURY

GINGER & GARLIC LICENSED RESTAURANT, 335 Stafford Street, Timaru, ph 03 688 3981

GREEN DOLPHIN RESTAURANT & BAR, 12 Avoca Street, Kaikoura, ph 03 319 6666

GRIMSBY'S RESTAURANT, Cranmer Court, cnr Kilmore & Montreal Streets, Christchurch, ph 03 379 2999

THE LYTTELTON BRASSERIE, 3 Norwich Quay, Lyttelton, ph 03 328 8841

MERCHANTS RESTAURANT, Hotel Grand Chancellor, 161 Cashel Street, Christchurch, ph 03 377 7457

THE OLD CONVENT, Mill Road, Kaikoura, ph 03 319 6603

CENTRAL OTAGO & FIORDLAND

BOARDWALK SEAFOOD RESTAURANT, Steamer Wharf, Queenstown, ph 03 442 5630

CAPRICCIO RESTAURANT, 123 Ardmore Street, Wanaka, ph 03 443 7085

CLANCY'S RESTAURANT, Lakeland Hotel, 14-18 Lake Esplanade, Queenstown, ph 03 442 7600

OLIVERS RESTAURANT & LODGE, 34 Sunderland Street, Clyde, ph 03 449 2860

RIPPLES RESTAURANT, Pembroke Mall, Wanaka, ph 03 443 7413

THE STABLES RESTAURANT & WINE BAR, 22 Buckingham Street, Arrowtown, ph 03 442 1818

SOUTHLAND & OTAGO

GERRARDS RESTAURANT, 3 Leven Street, Invercargill, ph 03 218 3406

LAST POST RESTAURANT, 12 Thames Street, Oamaru, ph 03 434 8080

NINETY FIVE, 95 Filleul Street, Dunedin, ph 03 471 9265

PALMS CAFÉ, 18 Queens Garden, Dunedin, ph 03 477 6534

TANGENTÉ BAKERY & CAFÉ, 111 Upper Moray Place, Dunedin, ph 03 477 0232

INDEX